# OLD MORMON NAUVOO
# AND SOUTHEASTERN IOWA

SECOND EDITION

# OLD MORMON
# NAUVOO
## AND
## SOUTHEASTERN IOWA

## HISTORIC PHOTOGRAPHS
## AND GUIDE

RICHARD NEITZEL HOLZAPFEL
and
T. JEFFERY COTTLE

1991
Fieldbrook Productions, Inc.

Book design by Richard Firmage.
Front and back cover photographs credited where they appear in the
text.

Library of Congress Catalog Number: 90–080906
ISBN: 1–879786–01–X

Printed in the United States of America

Fieldbrook Productions, Inc.
1901 E. Fourth Street, Suite 150
Santa Ana, California 92705

DEDICATED TO
THE MEN, WOMEN AND CHILDREN
WHO SETTLED EARLY NAUVOO
ON THE SESQUICENTENNIAL OF ITS FOUNDING
1989

# PREFACE

In September 1988, we visited Nauvoo to participate in the annual meeting of the John Whitmer Historical Association. While there, we took the customary tours of the historic sites in old Nauvoo. During this visit, we became aware of numerous other historic buildings that were in private possession, but found it difficult to locate many of them. We were also aware of several old photographs of Nauvoo that had been previously published in various articles and books; and we realized how interesting it would have been to have those photographs when we visited the sites.

Our effort to find specific places in Nauvoo and the surrounding communities grew into a year's work of merging the photographic record with written histories. We discovered that some of the identified historical sites did not match information available in contemporary journals or in early photographs. Over the years it has been claimed that so–and–so lived at a particular site or that this old photograph depicts the home of so–and–so. It has been difficult in some cases to decide which, if any, of the traditions about a site or photograph are true.

Years ago, Mr. W. C. Reimbold—so goes the story—collected antiques and sold them to visitors to Nauvoo. His specialties were old keys and antique beds, which he sold in great numbers, claiming they belonged to the Mormon prophet, Joseph Smith. Their uncertain histories make some of the photographs and sites in this book a little like the keys and beds sold by Mr. Reimbold.

The specific identification of several sites and photographs was challenging; we offer our results based on our comparison of panoramic views of the city with pictures and descriptions of individual sites, including some previously unpublished photographs. We also used land records, diaries, journals, census records and letters in our effort to establish a site. We welcome further research — even if it means revising our conclusions. Our initial conclusions were presented at a symposium entitled "Nauvoo — The City of Joseph" at Brigham Young University on 21 September 1989.

In this book we identify historic sites in the Nauvoo area, and provide a verbal and pictorial tour of each. As much as possible, we want visitors to Nauvoo to be able to visualize the city as it was built: each farm, house, and store a part of the "City of the Saints" that flourished for seven short years. The words of the builders help recapture the life of early Nauvoo, as do the photographs we've included. In quotations from journals, letters, and diary accounts, whether holographic writings or printed editions, we have often spelled out abbreviated words and modernized and made corrections in spelling and punctuation in order to help clarify the material. Brackets mark material we have inserted to make the quoted material more readable.

Many of the nineteenth and early twentieth century photographs in this guide are the earliest known photographs of their respective sites. Early photographs of some sites were not available, so we have used a few recent photographs. The endnotes and selected bibliography of published materials list additional sources of information about this important period in Nauvoo.

Many individuals have helped and encouraged us during our research and writing. Without their assistance this book would not have been possible. We thank Harold Allen, Dan Bachman, Alma Blair, Ruth Bywater, Dane Calkins, Lyndon Cook, Randy Dixon, Don Enders, Ron Esplin, Rell Francis, Steve Gardner, Bill Hartley, Genevieve Huffman, Brantley Jones, James Kimball, Stanley Kimball, Bill Knapp, Jess Kohlert, James Langenheim, Glen Leonard, Lillie McConkey, Kory Meyerick, Rowena Miller, Ron Romig, Bill Slaughter, Karen Seely, Genevieve Simmens, Steve Sorensen, Donna Taylor, Brad Westwood, and Buddy Youngreen. A special thanks to Camille Williams who was our primary editor and to Richard Firmage who designed the book.

Many institutions have graciously provided copies of photographs and permission to reproduce them. We thank the Brigham Young University Harold B. Lee Library Archives, The Church of Jesus Christ of Latter-day Saints Historical Department, the Missouri Historical

Society, the LDS Museum of Church History and Art, the Nauvoo Historical Society, the Historical Society of Quincy and Adams County, the Murphy Library at the University of Wisconsin, the Reorganized Church of Jesus Christ of Latter Day Saints Graphic Design Commission, the University of Utah Marriott Library and Archives, the U.S. Library of Congress, and the Utah State Historical Society. In making these acknowledgments, we nevertheless take full responsibility for the information contained herein.

Since 1989 is the sesquicentennial of both the founding of Nauvoo and the invention of photography we feel it especially appropriate to explore the city through that medium. This photographic essay is offered in the same spirit as Wilford Woodruff's parting plea:

> I left Nauvoo for the last time perhaps in this life. I looked upon the Temple and City of Nauvoo as I retired from it and felt to ask the Lord to preserve it as a monument of the sacrifice of his Saints.[1]

## NOTE TO THE SECOND EDITION

With the necessity of going back to press after the first printing of *Old Mormon Nauvoo* sold out, we have taken the opportunity to correct a few minor errors in the first edition and update information where it seemed necessary. We would also like to thank Ted D. Stoddard, Harold Allen and Elwin Robison for their suggestions regarding this edition.

# CONTENTS

# OLD MORMON NAUVOO AND SOUTHEASTERN IOWA

Aerial photo of Nauvoo. Notice Main Street begins and ends at the Mississippi River. Photograph courtesy of Utah State Historical Society.

# INTRODUCTION

Today a small town called Nauvoo lies tucked away in a little-known niche of western Illinois on the east bank of the Mississippi River. Nauvoo is about 185 miles north of St. Louis and 250 miles southwest of Chicago. For many visitors the name is just another among many on the Illinois State highway map. For those who are familiar with the history of Joseph Smith and the church he organized, the name has a special ring to it, a nostalgic ring, a historical ring. For others it is the name of a city now famous for its "Nauvoo Blue Cheese." The modern town of Nauvoo is located upon the bluffs which rise nearly seventy feet above the Mississippi River. To the west on the "flats" is the location of the historic city of Nauvoo as it was surveyed in the early part of the nineteenth century and built up by a unique American religious body, the Church of Jesus Christ of Latter-day Saints, known as the Mormons.

The Sac and Fox Indians maintained camps and trading posts along the Mississippi River as early as 1674. Modern Nauvoo itself was the site of an Indian village called Quashquema. In 1805 both tribes united and maintained a small village in the area. By 1826 there were almost five hundred members of the Sac-Fox tribe in the area. This Indian village was an important staging ground for hunting and fishing expeditions and an equally important agricultural site. The Indian men used canoes and dugouts to navigate the Mississippi for hunting and fishing. Wild deer, buffalo, turkey and fish were an important part of their diet, maize was grown, while maple syrup and honey, gathered together with wild grapes, rice and melons, allowed a good variety of food.

The Indians established a village near what would become Montrose, Lee County, Iowa. The expulsion of Indians from their Illinois villages in the 1820s led to the Black Hawk War in 1832 when Indians returned to Illinois attempting to retake their lands. It was already too late, the white settlement period had begun in western Illinois and eastern Iowa.

The cardinal feature of Illinois history, beginning in 1800, was the growth of white settlement. Throughout most of the eighteenth century the population, in large part French, increased slowly; but in the fall of 1779 an influx of new settlers began. The newcomers were Americans, mainly from Kentucky and Tennessee. Between 1800 and 1810, the population of Illinois grew to 12,282; in 1820 the federal census taker counted 55,211. Illinois became the twenty-first state in the Union on 3 December 1818. As the population expanded in the state, new settlements began to appear along the Mississippi River, including the present site of Nauvoo.

Traditionally, the Trading Oak in Nauvoo was identified as the place where Captain James White traded 200 bags of corn for the area known as Quashquema. White and his family are remembered in tradition as the first permanent white settlers in the area. Other settlers established homes and farms soon thereafter. Eventually, enough population growth in the area called for a reorganization of political boundaries.

Hancock County was organized in 1829 and a post office, called Venus, was established near the White home. This post office served two dozen families in the area by 1830. The village of Venus served as the first county seat of Hancock County; but the administration was subsequently moved to Carthage, which was the geographical center of the county. Venus continued to grow during this period.

Joseph B. Teas and Alexander White surveyed the land near Venus in 1834, and renamed the town Commerce. The small community served about a hundred farmers, merchants, and traders in the area. Several stores were established before the Mormons began to arrive at Commerce in May 1839. The first store was owned by Hiram Kimball and the second store was owned and operated by Amos Davis. Davis' store account book reveals important information regarding the extent of settlement in the area prior to the Mormon settlement—there were more settlers in the area than has been generally assumed in the past. The entire area along the Mississippi was being settled along with Commerce.

The new communities being established north of St. Louis were interconnected with each other mainly by steamboats. By 1829 some two hundred steamboats were in use on the Mississippi River. The river towns of Alton, Quincy, Warsaw, Commerce in Illinois and Keokuk and Montrose in Iowa were growing steadily. In 1835 more land was surveyed just north of Commerce and a second community was planned—its name was Commerce City. The Panic of 1837 slowed the sale of lots and property in Commerce and as a result the second city was never settled, it was a paper city.

The homes and businesses of early Commerce were scattered along the east banks of the Mississippi River for about one and a half miles. The Nauvoo of the Mormon period was a section of wilderness area made up of thickets and forest. Inland about a quarter of a mile was some rich farmland, some of which had been part of the earlier Indian agricultural settlement before the first white settler had arrived. Access to the town of Commerce was virtually impossible from these farmlands through the thickets, but farmers could have driven their wagons north to the Carthage Road and then westward to Commerce, which was located on the banks of the river.

In 1839 Isaac Galland was living in Commerce in the home of James White, which he had purchased some time during the winter. In the fall Galland met Israel Barlow, a Mormon who had recently arrived at Iowa from Missouri. This first contact with the Mormons would lead Galland to sell huge tracts of land to the destitute Saints at very reasonable terms.

Several members of the Mormon Church fled across the Mississippi River from the State of Missouri to Illinois during the winter of 1838–39. The citizens of Quincy, Adams County, Illinois opened their homes and offered assistance to these destitute people with extraordinary compassion. Even before the Saints came to Adams County, it was one of the largest population centers in the state, and Quincy, its county seat, was reputed to be one of the finer towns on the upper Mississippi River. In spite of the warm welcome and prospects available to the Saints in Adams County, they sought for another location to build a city. Mormon leaders decided to purchase land where they could build their own city.

In April 1839, Joseph Smith and other Mormon leaders escaped from jail in Liberty, Missouri, and headed east. They traveled incognito until joining friends and family in Quincy, Illinois. They had all been arrested in 1838 after surrendering the city of Far West, Missouri, the Mormon headquarters, to state militia leaders. Joseph had been sentenced to die, but several militia members, believing the execution would be illegal, vowed to keep him alive. Though Joseph was incarcerated in poor conditions for several months during the winter of 1838-1839, he remained the leader of his people, directing and counseling through letters to his family, friends, and the Church. Extracts from these letters were later canonized in the Nauvoo edition of the *Doctrine and Covenants*.

This was not the first time Joseph and his followers had suffered — they moved from New York to Ohio, to Missouri and then to Illinois in an effort to build God's kingdom on earth and to escape persecution. Joseph's vocation began during the religious ferment of the early 1800s, the Second Great Awakening, when heated evangelism spread, sweeping upper New York State with a special intensity.[1] In fact, revivals in this area west of the Catskill and Adirondack mountains were so constant and powerful that historians have labeled this ecclesiastical storm center the "Burned-over District."[2]

Joseph was born in Vermont in 1805; but in 1816 his family moved to New York, near the Finger Lakes region. In 1817 or 1818, he became concerned about religion and attended many open-air camp meetings and meetings of various churches in the area.[3] He was only fourteen when he experienced his first vision in the spring of 1820; in the following years he received a series of visions and angelic visitations.[4] He reported that in 1823 an angel directed him to a cache of metal plates containing the writings of some of the ancient inhabitants of the American continent. Joseph received the plates in 1827, translated them, and in March 1830 published the translation as the *Book of Mormon*.

Joseph was instructed by God not only to publish new scripture, but also to reestablish Christ's true church, which had been lost over time. Peter, James, and John, three of Jesus' original apostles, visited Joseph and a friend and ordained them to the priesthood of God. With this priesthood authority, Joseph organized the Church of Christ (the name was later changed) on 6 April 1830 in Fayette, New York.[5]

Additional revelations to the young prophet, collected and published in 1835, directed the Saints to build up Zion in America. The church grew both numerically and organizationally between 1830 and 1838. Joseph Smith was called of God to be the first elder, then president of the high priesthood. Twelve apostles were called as the church continued to grow in strength.

From the outset, the doctrines of Mormonism challenged the religious, social, economic, and political values of antebellum America. Although the United States had been a seedbed of religious dissent from the earliest colonial times, Joseph's critics were uneasy about a man who claimed continuing revelation and who introduced additional scripture. Their distaste for his doctrines became mixed with their fear of his power as believers flocked to him.

Missionary success in the Western Reserve area of Northern Ohio brought the Church and its prophet from New York to Kirtland, Ohio, in February 1831.[6] Many residents were awaiting the "restoration" of the original church of God, and they believed that Mormonism fulfilled their expectations. Establishing two Church headquarters, one in Ohio and the other in Missouri, Joseph sent missionaries throughout North America, and later to the British Isles. Converts were baptized and encouraged to gather with the Saints in Zion (Missouri) or in Ohio.

The small community of Kirtland, Ohio, swelled as members moved into the area. The Saints built their first temple there, dedicating it to God in March 1836. Within two years, contention among the Saints and conflict with their neighbors caused the prophet and other Church members to flee for safety. Traveling through Indiana and Illinois, they crossed the Mississippi River at Quincy, and made their way across the state of Missouri to Far West, an important Mormon community at the time. By mid-summer of 1838, most of the Saints had left the Kirtland area.

The original settlers of the Missouri and Ohio areas were alarmed by the influx of converts; with a significant missionary success rate (sometimes whole congregations converted), the Mormons became a threat to the social, religious, and economic stability of both areas. In Ohio and Missouri the Church encountered the full brunt of American intolerance. Episodes of violence were almost commonplace — tarrings, whippings, kidnappings, burnings, killings, imprisonments, and ultimately the expulsion of the body of the Church from Missouri under the "Extermination Order" of Governor Lilburn W. Boggs.

The violence in Missouri increased with the blessing of the state. In October 1838, David Patten, one of the Twelve Apostles, was shot and killed at the Battle of Crooked River. A few days later, on the afternoon of Tuesday, 30 October, Missouri militia troops attacked the settlement at Haun's Mill. Eighteen Mormons were savagely killed, and as many as fifteen others were severely wounded.[7]

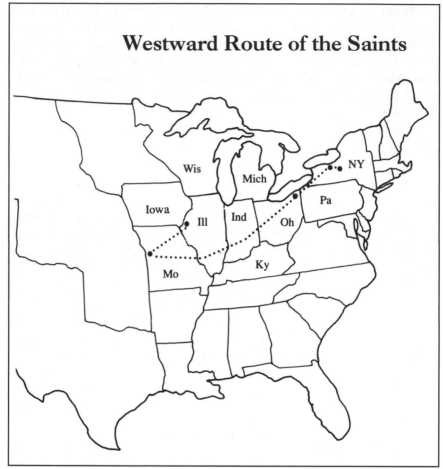

# Westward Route of the Saints

Map of westward route of the Mormons (Church of Jesus Christ of Latter-day Saints) from New York to Illinois.

In late January 1839, Apostle Brigham Young took almost four hundred Mormons back across the Mississippi River to Illinois and Iowa seeking refuge from the mobs and state militia in northern Missouri. They found temporary safety along the river in Quincy, Illinois, and at the abandoned Fort Des Moines in Iowa. The people of Quincy helped the Saints with earnest sympathy. Food and shelter were supplied, and Joseph's wife, Emma, and her family found a place to stay in the home of John and Sarah Cleveland, some three miles from Quincy.

Parley P. Pratt, one of the Church leaders who remained in Missouri under arrest, described his escape across the river to the safety of the Illinois shore:

> I then descended from the height and entered the town . . . I examined the shore and soon convinced myself that no public ferry was kept there. I was extremely glad to learn this fact — being fully aware that by this time all the ferries would be watched. . . . We soon landed in the woods in a low bottom, with no sign of inhabitants, although while crossing I had seen some houses on the shore a mile or two below. I now paid the boy his dollar, and he pushed off and commenced his way back exceedingly well pleased. I immediately stepped a few paces into the woods, and kneeling down kissed the ground as a land of liberty, and then poured out my soul in thanks to God.[8]

Eventually other Church leaders including Joseph Smith escaped incarceration in Missouri and fled to Illinois. After joining his family in Quincy, the fugitive prophet looked again for a gathering place, this time in Iowa and Illinois. The river towns of Commerce in Illinois and Montrose in Iowa had grown steadily in the 1820s; Commerce appeared a promising place for the resettlement of the Saints.

The homes and businesses of early Commerce were scattered along the east bank of the Mississippi River for about one and a half miles. Land was cheap enough, and settlement sparse enough, that new Mormon communities could be organized in Hancock County, Illinois, and in Lee County, Iowa. The founding of Nauvoo, which Joseph Smith said meant "the City Beautiful," began with Joseph and his family moving to Commerce in 1839. The word "Nauvoo" was derived from the Hebrew word for "beautiful."

On the bend of the river: Nauvoo. Photograph courtesy of Harold Allen.

Nauvoo was planned and built to be the new Church center, with an additional seventeen communities planned for Hancock County. Joseph envisioned Nauvoo encircled by smaller settlements. On 1 March 1843 the Prophet explained: "There is a wheel; Nauvoo is the hub; we will drive the first spoke in Ramus (Webster), second in La Harpe, third Shokoquon, forth in Lima: that is half the wheel. The other half is over the river."[9]

# EARLY NAUVOO, 1839–1846

On 27 April 1844, Lucian Foster arrived in Nauvoo from New York. He was accompanied by Hiram Clark and one hundred fifty Saints from Liverpool, England.[1] The city with its young prophet looked like an attractive place to do business. When Foster arrived in Nauvoo, he saw a pleasant, prosperous, well-planned city. Log cabins were numerous, but a considerable number of brick and plank houses were shifting the settlement from frontier to city status. The Nauvoo Temple overlooking the Mississippi and the Nauvoo House, a Church-sponsored hotel, were under construction.

Nauvoo was alive with dinner parties, Christmas celebrations, quilting bees, house-raisings, cornhusking parties, a circus, Fourth of July celebrations, military parades, reenactments of famous battles in American history and summer swims in the Mississippi. The *Maid of Iowa*, a steamboat owned by Captain Dan Jones and later by the Church, was used for excursions on the Mississippi.[2] Many a Saturday afternoon was spent in competitive jumping, pulling sticks, running, throwing weights, and wrestling. During the winter, the Saints enjoyed sliding on the frozen river.

The Prophet Joseph Smith was a significant part of the life of the city. He was the presiding elder and mayor, a fellow skater and ball-player. Mosiah Hancock played ball with him and recorded: "We took turns knocking and chasing the ball."[3] "At 4 P.M. went out with Frederick [Smith] to slide on the ice," Joseph noted in his journal on Wednesday, 11 February 1842[4]; under the date of 18 March 1843 he wrote, "In the afternoon rode out . . . about 4 [o'clock] to a game of ball east of Main street."[5]

Nauvoo from Montrose. Photograph courtesy of Utah State Historical Society.

Joseph was the main reason Nauvoo grew. Convert and curious came to him, and he welcomed them. For many of the Saints arriving in Nauvoo, this was their first opportunity to see a large gathering of Church members, and their first experience with the Prophet himself. William Clayton wrote home a few days after his arrival in Nauvoo with two hundred other British Saints: "We have had the privilege of conversing with Joseph Smith Jr. and we are delighted with his company." Clayton continued:

> He is not an idiot, but a man of sound judgment, and possessed of abundance of intelligence and whilst you listen to his conversation you receive intelligence which expands your mind and causes your heart to rejoice.

Clayton's letter describes a growing city—promising, but not yet Zion:

> There has been a great influx of Saints this year. . . . the houses are built of wood, and each house has an acre of land to it. There is space left for streets apparently from 10 to 15 yards wide. There are houses belonging to the Saints for several miles round. . . . There are some who are not good Saints and some very good ones.[6]

By the summer of 1841 there were between eight and nine thousand Saints in the Nauvoo area. Within another year, Nauvoo had

Shoreline, Water St. and Aaron Johnson Home. Photograph courtesy of RLDS Graphic Design Commission.

eclipsed every other Illinois city in size, with the possible exception of Chicago. Almost single-handedly, the Saints made Hancock County the most populous county in Illinois by the 1845 census.

Like others who came to Nauvoo, Lucian Foster wanted to do more than see the city. He wanted to meet the man who had seen God, and been commissioned to build Zion. He visited Joseph Smith on 29 April 1844, and presented the prophet a gold pencil case sent by Theodore Curtis, a Church member in New York. The prophet used the pencil to write "God bless the man."[7] Foster soon took up residence in the Mansion House. He had served as president of the New York Branch of the Mormon Church from 1841 until shortly before he left for Illinois, so he was familiar with the struggles of the fledgling church.

Proselyting missions to the Lamanites (the Mormon name for native Americans) began very early in the 1830s and continued during the Nauvoo period. Mormons believed the Indians were descendants of Israelites who had settled the Americas before the time of Christ. Some Sac, Fox, Potawatomi, and other Indians visited Church leaders in Nauvoo during the 1840s.[8] A few joined the Church and moved to Nauvoo to live with the Saints.

Missionary work was only moderately successful among the Lamanites, but was astonishingly successful among other groups, especially in the British Isles. Hundreds, then thousands, listened and believed the husbands, fathers, brothers, and sons sent from Nauvoo to gather the faithful. Mormon women kept the faith at home, providing for their families and fighting the loneliness of separations lasting anywhere from several months to several years. Bathsheba Smith wrote her husband, George Albert, on 16 July 1843:

> I wish I could have been with you and stayed until you started, for it seemed such a long time until the boat came. I thought perhaps you would come home again in a few minutes, but I was disappointed. I wanted to see you very much. I would have gone to you if I could. O my dear it is nothing to cry when one feels as I did when I saw the boat going down [the river]. I was pleased to think you would not have to wait any longer, but then how could I bare to have it carry you off so rapidly from me. I watched it until I could not see it any longer then I held my head for it ached. Soon your father and mother came in. George A. cries, "pa." He feels bad [and] wants to see you. He often goes to the door to see you. When we say, "where is father?" he will say, "a da pa."[9]

The bitterness of such departures made reunion sweet. Eliza R. Snow wrote of her brother's return from a mission to England:

> This day I have the inexpressible happiness of once again embracing a brother who had been absent nearly three years. I cannot describe the feelings which filled my bosom when I saw the steam-boat Amaranth moving majestically up the Mississippi, and thought perhaps Lorenzo was on board; my heart overflowed with gratitude when, after the landing of the boat, I heard Pres. Hyrum Smith say to me "your brother has actually arrived." It is a time of mutual rejoicing which I never shall forget.[10]

Many of the converts who came to Nauvoo were faithful, but were unprepared for the pioneer lifestyle. Joseph Smith wrote to the Twelve Apostles in England on 15 December 1840, outlining his concerns that emigration procedures be sensible:

> I would likewise observe that inasmuch as this place has been appointed for the gathering of the Saints, it is necessary that it should be attended to, in the order which the Lord intends it should; to this end I would say that as there are great numbers of the Saints in

England, who are extremely poor and not accustomed to the farming business, who must have certain preparations made for them before they can support themselves in this country, therefore to prevent confusion and disappointment when they arrive here, let those men who are accustomed to making machinery and those who can command a capital even if it be but small, come here as soon as convenient and put up machinery and make such other preparation as may be necessary, so that when the poor come on they may have employment to come to.[11]

Unlike some who came with few skills, Foster brought with him the equipment for daguerreotypy, (the earliest photographic process) and some skill in that new science of image making. The *Nauvoo Neighbor* dated 10 August 1844 carried his advertisement to make "an image of the person, as exact as that formed by the mirror, that is transferred to, and permanently fixed upon a highly polished silver plate, through the agency of an optical instrument."[12]

The same paper that carried Foster's ad carried advertisements for merchants selling shoes, bonnets, and patent medicines; it listed the services of lawyers, real estate agents, book binders, and teachers. The growth of the nation was reflected in the growth of such newspapers: between 1830 and 1840 the number of papers published jumped from eight hundred to more than fourteen hundred. Nauvoo itself saw the

Main Street looking north. Photograph courtesy of LDS Historical Department.

establishment of several newspapers, including the *Times and Seasons,
Wasp, Nauvoo Neighbor*, and the *Nauvoo Expositor.*

The *Wasp* began publication on 16 April 1842 under the editor-
ship of William Smith, Joseph's younger brother. This weekly pro-
moted agriculture, art, commerce, literature, science, trade, and included
some general news. It was also a vehicle for the Church to respond to
anti-Mormon attacks, allowing the *Times and Seasons* to focus on Church
history. That paper began the publication of a long series of articles
prepared by Joseph Smith on the history of his revelations and the
early history of the Church. These articles are the basis for the multi-
volume LDS Church's *History of the Church*.[13] The *Times and Seasons*
did not become a religious paper like each of its predecessors.

Nauvoo newspapers not only chronicled commercial enterprise,
but also family tragedy: "Drowned — In this city July 23rd, Samuel W.
aged 8 years, and James F. C. aged 6 years both children of Stephen
and Mary Luce, formerly of Maine." [14]

While these published accounts announced public information, private journals spoke of the personal sorrows. The ague — malaria, with
its chills and fever — took many lives before the swampland was drained,

Main Street looking south. Photograph courtesy of Harold Allen.

and the anopheles mosquito, carrier of that meanest of all diseases, was somewhat controlled. Sally Randall was one who wrote about the sickness in the city:

> October 6, 1843
> Dear Friends. . . . we landed in Nauvoo on the 22 [September 1843] about 2 o'clock in the morning. I found James [her husband] in as good health and circumstances as I expected. He has a lot with a log cabin on it. . . . It is very sickly here at present with fevers, ague, and measles. A great many children die with them.

Four weeks later, Sally wrote of her own personal grief:

> November 12 [1843]
> Dear Friends. . . . George [her son] has gone to try the realities of eternity. He died the first day of this month about 3 o'clock in the morning. He was sick three weeks and three days with ague and fever . . . he was taken in fits the day before he died and had them almost without cessation as long as he lived. When he breathed his last he went very easy, but oh the agonies he was in before it seemed I could not endure.[15]

The Saints turned to God for help during such tragedies. In her journal, Zina Jacobs remembered the dying children, and prayed on 7 August 1845:

> Disease continues to prey upon the children. O Lord how long shall we labor under these things, even children suffering so sore? Wilt thou hasten the time in thine own way when the Saints shall have power over the destroyer of our mortal body. Not that I would complain at thy hard dealings, O Lord. All things are right with Thee. But, oh the weakness of human nature.[16]

Many Saints left their goods in Missouri and came to Illinois with few resources. Many were impoverished and ill. Some died from exhaustion, some from hunger, some in childbirth or in accidents. The lifeless little body of Marian Lyon, a child of Windsor and Sylvia Lyon, was presented to Joseph on the stand during a church service. According to a contemporary diary:

> A young child was dead and his corpse presented in the assembly it called for many remarks from the speaker upon death. . . . the only difference between the old and young dying is one lives longer in heaven and eternal light and glory than the other and was freed a little sooner from this miserable wicked world.[17]

Death was an occasion for learning about God. King Follett died on 9 March 1844 while walling up a well. A rope broke, letting a bucket of rock fall and crush him. At Follett's funeral, death was not characterized as a dark, unknown, fearful thing. The Prophet comforted the Saints with his vision of the next life:

> I call the attention of this congregation while I address you upon the subject of the dead. The case of our beloved brother King Follett, who was crushed to death in a well, as well as many others who have lost friends will be had in mind this afternoon. . . . you mourners have occasion to rejoice for your husband has gone to wait until the redemption and your expectations and hopes are far above what man can conceive—for why God has revealed to us and I am authorized to say by the authority of the Holy Ghost that you have no occasion to fear for he is gone to the home of the just—don't mourn don't weep.[18]

In that same address—the King Follett Discourse—Joseph Smith articulated the Mormon doctrine of deity and eternal progression.[19] In his Nauvoo sermons, Joseph expanded upon many of the teachings introduced to the Church during the years in Missouri and Ohio. Many of his public sermons were delivered in a grove on a slope below the rising temple at Nauvoo.[20] Some doctrines he taught privately to a select group of disciples who made those teachings public only after his death in 1844.[21]

Lucian Foster had arrived in Nauvoo just after Joseph's 7 April 1844 general conference address on the nature of God. He must have been aware of increasing division among Church members concerning Joseph and his teachings. William Law, formerly a member of the Church's First Presidency, reacted negatively:

> Conference is over, and some of the most blasphemous doctrines have been taught by J. Smith and others ever heard of . . . It was a strange Conference, was not organized at all, and was managed in a most unprecedented manner.[22]

While Law rejected Joseph and the doctrine, others responded favorably. Wilford Woodruff reported a significant amount of the discourse in his journal, commenting: "3 o'clock p.m. April Sunday 7th 1844. The following important, edifying, and interesting discourse was delivered by President Joseph Smith."[23]

Joseph Fielding considered the conference a positive witness of Joseph Smith's call. He wrote in April 1844:

Looking toward the "flats" from "upper" Nauvoo. Photograph courtesy of LDS Historical Department.

As to me I have evidence enough that Joseph is not fallen, I have seen him . . . organize the Kingdom of God [Council of Fifty] on earth and am myself a member of it in this I feel myself highly honored but feel grieved that at this time of greatest light and the greatest glory and honor, men of so much knowledge and understanding, should cut themselves off [William and Wilson Law] . . . Our annual conference began and continued four days. Joseph's discourse on the origin of man, the nature of God, and the resurrection was the most interesting matter of this time and any one that could not see in him the spirit of inspiration of God must be dark, they might have known that he was not a fallen Prophet even if they thought he was fallen.[24]

Lucian Foster set up shop when the city of Nauvoo was expanding; he would first see Joseph, then the city itself, fall victim to dissent and violence. It may have been during this time that Foster photographed the prophet-statesman. According to Joseph's son, Foster made a daguerreotype of Joseph, an image that has been photographically copied and published numerous times.[25] Although this remembrance has not been substantiated and records of Foster's work are incomplete, he was apparently the first to photograph scenes in Nauvoo.

Before Joseph Smith's murder, Foster was actively involved in the civic affairs in the city, including Joseph Smith's presidential candidacy. This work included his appointment to the central committee in charge of coordinating Joseph's national campaign.

View of Nauvoo, looking south from the temple site. Photograph courtesy of RLDS Graphic Design Commission.

Foster's work in Nauvoo not only included photographing the prominent city buildings but also making individual and family portraits. While life in Nauvoo drastically changed as the result of the tragic events of the prophet's death 27 June 1844, life nevertheless moved forward. On 23 August 1844 Wilford Woodruff recorded the following: "Mrs. Woodruff and myself visited Brother and Sister Stoddard and Brother and Sister Foster and obtained our miniatures by the ingenuity of Brother Foster at [by] the apparatus of his daguerreotype. We both obtained a good likeness . . . "[26]

During the next two years Nauvoo continued to grow and eventually was renamed by Mormons the City of Joseph, in honor of their martyred prophet.

Sometime before March 1845, Foster moved his gallery from the Mansion House to Parley Street. The spring and summer of 1845 was a busy time for the Saints. Work on the temple moved forward with renewed energy as the Saints committed themselves to fulfilling Joseph's vision and mission at Nauvoo. Like so many others, Foster occupied himself with his own work simultaneously with his work in the community and Church. In March 1845 he was busy photographing mem-

Heber John, Willard, and Jennetta Richards at Nauvoo.
Photograph courtesy of LDS Historical Department.

bers of the community. On 17 March, Hosea Stout noted in his diary the following: "in the forenoon went to Foster and had him take a daguerreotype likeness of myself."[27] A few days later, on 26 March, Willard Richards wrote in his diary: "10 a.m. went to Foster's, daguerreotype with Jennetta and Heber John."[28]

In the fall and winter of 1845, the Saints made a last concentrated effort to finish the temple. At this time, Foster, like many members of the Church, received his temple ordinances. He also served as a clerk in the temple beginning on 27 December 1845.

Shortly thereafter, the temple and city were abandoned by the Saints as they began their trek west. It was during this time that Foster probably took the photograph of Nauvoo with the temple on a distant hill. He must have taken it from somewhere near his gallery on Parley Street, looking toward the completed temple. This haunting view shows neither saint nor sinner: no skaters, no animals, no people stiffly posed for history; in fact, the city looks empty. Another Foster photograph is a close-up of the temple.

On 3 April 1846, Foster advertised his services for the last time in Hancock County.[29] For some unknown reason, Foster did not go west.

Eventually he returned to New York; but the photographs he left show something of his experience in Nauvoo.

Since the daguerreotype was introduced in 1839, photographers have been preserving the past through its unique medium. The invention of modern photography helped freeze Nauvoo's past in time. Few photographs of Nauvoo taken in the 1840s or 1850s exist, but many photographs taken in the late nineteenth and early twentieth centuries

"Temple on the hill from the flats" (see Appendix 3). Daguerreotype courtesy of LDS Historical Department.

have been preserved. These invaluable historic documents depict many buildings from the Mormon period that have disappeared.

Thomas M. Easterly's close-up of the temple may have been taken as early as 1846, and is the third known photograph of historic Nauvoo. Easterly, a St. Louis photographer, was active in and around St. Louis in the late 1840s and 1850s. In 1850, T.W. Cox made a tintype of the front of the Nauvoo Temple clearly showing the damage from the fire in 1848. These four photographs constitute the only known pictures of the city of the Saints taken in the 1840s and 1850s. Others may exist, but are currently undiscovered or unrecognized.

The next chronicler of Mormon Nauvoo may have been B.H. Roberts, LDS Church leader and historian, who visited Illinois in 1885 on his way home from the Southern States Mission. Several of his photographs have appeared in church and scholarly publications. A minor difficulty with the Roberts collection is the specific identification of some sites. Roberts, who never lived in Nauvoo, relied heavily on information obtained from Mayor M. M. Morrill, a Nauvoo resident. Some of the photographs are mislabeled because Roberts relied

Upper Nauvoo, Mulholland Street. Photograph courtesy of LDS Historical Department.

on local traditions concerning these sites instead of searching records to verify the accuracy of the traditions.[30]

George Edward Anderson, a Utah portrait and landscape photographer, may have been the next important individual who worked to preserve Nauvoo's history in photographs. Anderson's mission to England allowed him time to visit and photograph many of the Church historical sites in the spring of 1907. He arrived in Nauvoo on 2 May 1907 and recorded in his journal:

> Visited the most interesting points, old homes of the Saints, the Prophet's home, Temple ground. In the afternoon made views of the most prominent places. Brother Pitt rowed Ida Alleman and Sister Bennion across the river to Bluff Park, Iowa side, and got a beautiful view of Nauvoo. Enjoyed the ride very much. Made a view of the grave of Emma Smith Bidamon, . . . Nauvoo Mansion, Nauvoo House, and many things that brought to ruin the condition of our Temple sixty years ago.[31]

Anderson's photographs are in several collections in a variety of public institutions, as well as in private hands. Therefore, a number of his pictures of Nauvoo remain uncatalogued and unpublished. The sequential numbers on his glass plates indicate that he took more photographs of the Nauvoo area than are presently known, so it is possible that more of his plates will be located. Like the Roberts' collection, some of his photographs have been mislabeled when published.

The Ida Blum collection, housed at the Harold B. Lee Library Archives at Brigham Young University, contains numerous photographs of Nauvoo. Unfortunately these photographs are uncatalogued and have sometimes been mislabeled, the mislabeling perpetuating inaccurate information about the city.

The Harold Allen collection, in private possession, contains photographs taken by several Nauvoo residents, including Sam Strange. This collection also contains photographs by Mr. Allen beginning in 1951 before any major restoration.

Several members of the Mormon and Reorganized churches (both groups view Joseph Smith as founder) visited Nauvoo and recorded in words and photographs the historic section of town. Many buildings from the Mormon period were ruined, abandoned, or destroyed before these individuals visited the city; however, their visits helped preserve knowledge about old Nauvoo.[32]

# NAUVOO TODAY

Modern Nauvoo is located on bluffs nearly seventy feet above the Mississippi River. "Upper" Nauvoo has unique shops, restaurants, and overnight accommodations, as well as a Nauvoo Visitors and Information Center. Religious belief is still important to its citizens: its several churches include the Christ Lutheran Church, the Peter and Paul Catholic Church, the United Methodist Church, the Presbyterian Church, The Church of Jesus Christ of Latter-day Saints (LDS), and the Reorganized Church of Jesus Christ of Latter Day Saints (RLDS) as well as Saint Mary's Boarding School for Girls and Saint Mary Priory.

To the west, on the "flats," is the location of the historic city of Nauvoo as it was surveyed and built by the Mormons a century and a half ago. While much of that city no longer exists, some portions of it can be seen today.

The Mormons originally laid out orderly streets with large lots. Driving those streets now, it is possible to sense their effort to erect hundreds of buildings: new homes, shops, schools, and businesses. At first, many homes were simple log cabins or homes made of lumber rafted from Wisconsin. Thomas Gregg, a Warsaw, Illinois, newspaper editor, said that during the heyday the Saints at Nauvoo built about 1,200 hand-hewn log cabins, most of them whitewashed inside, and 300 to 500 frame homes. Using brick and lime made in their own kilns, the Mormons erected 200 to 300 good, substantial brick homes.

The architectural style of these homes often reflected the owners' place of origin. Former New Englanders favored neat Federal style homes while most New Yorkers preferred the Greek Revival style.

The Federalist style, created by 1776 in Scotland (it was known as Adamesques in Europe), was readily accepted in the United States and is called Federal because it was used during the early period of the new nation. Many homes in Nauvoo often used the primarily square or rectangular shape of the Federalist style.³³

A significant number of Nauvoo homes were built in the Greek Revival style, which often incorporated Greek-inspired columns and pilasters. Other easily identifiable features included bold, simple moldings on both the exterior and interior, and the lack of arched entrances and fan windows so common to the Federal style. Many structures using the Greek Revival style were built in Europe, but in the United States during the 1830s and 1840s the style flourished like nowhere else in the world. This style became so widespread it was known as the national style.

Many historic Nauvoo homes combine a variety of styles, and as such are hard to label. Nearly all of the brick homes built by the Mormons, however, were practical, boxlike structures with gable roofs and single or double brick chimneys built into the end walls. (See Appendix 2 for a further discussion and photographs of architecture in Nauvoo.)

The most important structure in Nauvoo was located on the hill overlooking the Mississippi, crowning the city of homes, businesses, and public buildings—the beautiful Nauvoo Temple. It was built of native gray limestone and pine from Wisconsin. From its tower the whole region—fields, farms, orchards, and woods—could be seen.

After most of the Mormons left, others came to claim the land and the city. A French Icarian group came to Nauvoo in March 1849 to set up a communal living experiment. The "Pioneers of Humanity" numbered about two hundred eighty and were under the leadership of Etienne Cabet. Nauvoo was ideal for them since homes and land were plentiful and in many cases could be had by paying the back taxes. A newspaper was established—first called the *Popular Tribune*, later called the *Nauvoo Herald*. By 14 January 1851, the community numbered three hundred thirty-five individuals. Most of these members were French socialists, though there were some natives of Holland, Germany, Poland, and Switzerland. This community flourished for several years, but by the late 1850s internal strife divided the population of approximately five hundred. The society moved to a site near Corning, Iowa.

As the Icarian period was waning, English, Irish, German, and Swiss emigrants began to settle in the area. It was in "upper" Nauvoo that the new town center took shape while the historic area fell into ruin.

Shortly after the Mormon exodus in 1846, J. H. Buckingham, a gentleman from Boston, visited the abandoned "flats" of historic Nauvoo, expressing the reactions of many visitors of the last century, and of our own time:

> the rise and progress of Nauvoo, will be, if it should ever be written, a romance of thrilling interest. No one can visit Nauvoo, and come away without a conviction that . . . the body of the Mormons were an industrious, hard-working, and frugal people. In the history of the whole world there cannot be found such another instance of so rapid a rise of a city out of the wilderness—a city so well built, a territory so well cultivated. . . . Joe Smith, the Prophet-leader, was, although an uneducated man, a man of great power, and a man who could conceive great projects.[34]

Mr. Buckingham's feelings about the city, its inhabitants, and its prophet are echoed not only by those who visit it for a few hours or days, but also by those who have spent years restoring it.

Several groups have made Nauvoo one of the largest and finest historic preservation sites in mid-America. The Department of Commerce and Community Affairs for the state of Illinois, the Illinois State Historical Society, the LDS Church through the work of Nauvoo Restoration, Inc., the National Park Service, the Nauvoo Historical Society, the Nauvoo Tourism Board, the Office of Tourism, and the RLDS Church have all contributed to this restoration project.

Visitors today see some homes restored to their 1840s appearance. While it is virtually impossible to recreate the physical past, the restoration of old Nauvoo preserves some of that past for present and future visitors to admire. The buildings that are open for visitors include the homes of Joseph Smith, the Homestead and the Mansion House; the home of Sarah Melissa Granger Kimball, one of the original members of the Female Relief Society of Nauvoo; the home of Brigham Young, leader of the Mormon trek west; and the home of Jonathan Browning, gunsmith and inventor. Public buildings and businesses, such as the Printing Office Complex and Cultural Hall, are also open to the public. Joseph Smith's Red Brick Store and the Webb Wagon and Blacksmith Shop have been reconstructed and sit upon their original foundations.

Early nineteenth century crafts have been revitalized and are demonstrated daily for those visiting the historic area. The LDS and the

RLDS churches have constructed beautiful visitors' centers that provide information about the city's history. Both interpret their respective histories and their ongoing stories in light of the events in Nauvoo during the Mormon period. The historic city of Nauvoo offers numerous free tours, horse and carriage rides, and craft demonstrations, though hours are restricted in winter.

This book includes maps of each section of the city, with directions to each historic site. The city has been divided into nine separate areas beginning with the temple area or "upper" Nauvoo, the center of the modern town. The early photographs will help you visualize historic Nauvoo which has long since disappeared, while the excerpts from the contemporary accounts and reminiscences of former inhabitants of old Nauvoo will help you expand your understanding of the people who lived there. Symbols (*, O, or □) placed above each place heading in the Guided Tours section are keyed to the maps and allow the reader at a glance to know whether the structure mentioned is actually still existing and if it is open to public tours.

The final section of this book, "Guided Tours of the Surrounding Communities," discusses Carthage, Webster (Ramus), Warsaw, Morley's Settlement, Lima, Quincy, and Montrose and Sugar Creek (both in Iowa), and their relationship to the settlement of Nauvoo. That section begins with a map of the entire area, and includes a short account of events at those historical sites. For some of the sites a photograph is included.

# GUIDED TOURS

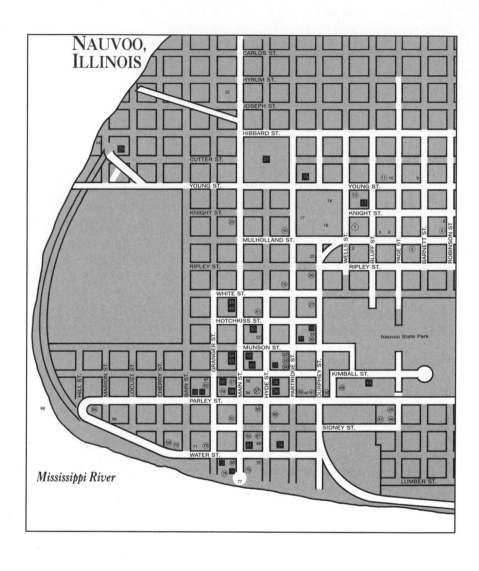

NAUVOO,
ILLINOIS

CARLOS ST.

HYRUM ST.

JOSEPH ST.

HIBBARD ST.

CUTTER ST.

YOUNG ST.

YOUNG ST.

KNIGHT ST.

KNIGHT ST.

MULHOLLAND ST.

RIPLEY ST.

RIPLEY ST.

WHITE ST.

HOTCHKISS ST.

MUNSON ST.

KIMBALL ST.

SIDNEY ST.

PARLEY ST.

WATER ST.

LUMBER ST.

*Mississippi River*

Nauvoo State Park

HILL ST.
MARION ST.
LOCUST ST.
CHERRY ST.
BAIN ST.
GRANGER ST.
MAIN ST.
HYDE ST.
PARTRIDGE ST.
DURPHEY ST.

WELLS ST.
BLUFF ST.
PAGE ST.
BARNETT ST.
ROBINSON ST.

1. Temple Site
2. Amos Davis
3. Robert Foster
4. Expositor
5. Nauvoo Historical
6. Joseph Agnew
7. East Grove
8. Charles Rich
9. Howard Coray
10. Orson Spencer
11. James Hendricks
12. Raymond Clark
13. Parley P. Pratt
14. Arsenal
15. William Weeks
16. West Grove
17. Edward Hunter
18. William Gheen
19. David Yearsley
20. Hosea Stout
21. L.D.S. Visitors Center
22. Temple Quarry
23. Sarah G. Kimball
24. Hiram Kimball
25. Elijah Malin
26. Jacob Weiler
27. Jennetta Richards
28. Wilford Woodruff
29. Lorin Farr
30. Winslow Farr

31. Heber C. Kimball
32. Porter Rockwell
33. Samuel Williams
34. Silas Condit
35. Brickyard
36. Noble-Smith
37. Snow-Ashby
38. Joseph Coolidge
39. Newel K. Whitney
40. Thomas Moore
41. John Smith
42. Drainage Ditch
43. Sunstone
44. Nauvoo Museum
45. George Laub
46. Ellis Sanders
47. William Mendenhall
48. Cultural Hall
49. Scovil Bakery
50. Lyon Drug
51. Orson Hyde
52. John D. Lee
53. Jonathan Browning
54. Sylvester Stoddard
55. Printing Complex
56. Widow's Row
57. Vinson Knight
58. George C. Riser
59. John Taylor
60. Brigham Young

61. Joseph Young
62. Chancey Webb
63. Webb Blacksmith
64. Seventies Hall
65. Exodus Monument
66. James White
67. Island
68. Wilson Law
69. Jonathan Wright
70. Arron Johnson
71. Times & Seasons
72. William Marks
73. Red Brick Store
74. R.L.D.S. Visitor Center
75. Joseph Smith Stable
76. Nauvoo House
77. Nauvoo House Dock
78. Homestead
79. Cemetery
80. Survey Stone
81. Mansion House
82. Sidney Rigdon
83. City Hotel
84. Butler Store
85. Simeon Dunn
86. Henry Thomas
87. Hiram Clark
88. Theodore Turley
89. Calvin Pendleton

# KEY

2 No Present Standing Structure
5 Standing Structure or Marker
12 Standing Structure—Open to the Public

2. Amos Davis
3. Robert Foster
4. Expositor
7. East Grove
8. Charles Rich
9. Howard Coray
10. Orson Spencer
14. Arsenal
16. West Grove
17. Edward Hunter
22. Temple Quarry
24. Hiram Kimball
25. Elijah Malin
29. Lorin Farr
40. Thomas Moore
52. John D. Lee
56. Widow's Row
61. Joseph Young
66. James White
67. Island
68. Wilson Law
71. Times & Seasons
75. Joseph Smith Stable
77. Nauvoo House Dock
84. Butler Store
88. Theodore Turley

(1) Temple Site

(5) Nauvoo Historical

(6) Joseph Agnew

(11) James Hendricks

(13) Parley P. Pratt

(18) William Gheen

(19) David Yearsley

(20) Hosea Stout

(26) Jacob Weiler

(27) Jennetta Richards

(30) Winslow Farr

(32) Porter Rockwell

(33) Samuel Williams

(34) Silas Condit

(37) Snow-Ashby

(39) Newel K. Whitney

(41) John Smith

(42) Drainage Ditch

(43) Sunstone

(45) George Laub

(46) Ellis Sanders

(47) William Mendenhall

(51) Orson Hyde

(57) Vinson Knight

(59) John Taylor

(62) Chancey Webb

(65) Exodus Monument

(69) Jonathan Wright

(70) Arron Johnson

(72) William Marks

(76) Nauvoo House

(79) Cemetery

(80) Survey Stone

(82) Sidney Rigdon

(83) City Hotel

(85) Simeon Dunn

(86) Henry Thomas

(87) Hiram Clark

12 Raymond Clark

15 William Weeks

21 L.D.S. Visitors Center

23 Sarah G. Kimball

28 Wilford Woodruff

31 Heber C. Kimball

35 Brickyard

36 Noble-Smith

38 Joseph Coolidge

44 Nauvoo Museum

48 Cultural Hall

49 Scovil Bakery

50 Lyon Drug

53 Jonathan Browning

54 Sylvester Stoddard

55 Printing Complex

58 George C. Riser

60 Brigham Young

63 Webb Blacksmith

64 Seventies Hall

73 Red Brick Store

74 R.L.D.S. Visitor Center

78 Homestead

81 Mansion House

89 Calvin Pendleton

# KEY

2  No Present Standing Structure
(5) Standing Structure or Marker
12 Standing Structure—Open to the Public

# Upper Nauvoo

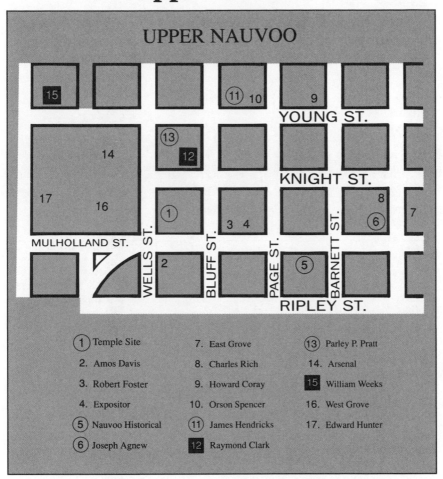

UPPER NAUVOO

YOUNG ST.

KNIGHT ST.

MULHOLLAND ST.

WELLS ST.

BLUFF ST.

PAGE ST.

BARNETT ST.

RIPLEY ST.

1. Temple Site
2. Amos Davis
3. Robert Foster
4. Expositor
5. Nauvoo Historical
6. Joseph Agnew
7. East Grove
8. Charles Rich
9. Howard Coray
10. Orson Spencer
11. James Hendricks
12. Raymond Clark
13. Parley P. Pratt
14. Arsenal
15. William Weeks
16. West Grove
17. Edward Hunter

Nauvoo Temple.  Daguerreotype courtesy of LDS Historical Department.

O *

# 1. THE NAUVOO TEMPLE SITE

The Nauvoo Temple was built on the east side of Wells between Mulholland and Knight streets. Nonextant three-story gray limestone and white pine lumber building similar in style to the first Mormon temple at Kirtland, Ohio, but with Greek Revival proportions.[1]

## Historical Background

Joseph Smith's public announcement of the construction of the Nauvoo Temple on 3 October 1840 started the work that occupied the Saints until they left the city in 1846. However, it was a revelation (LDS *Doctrine & Covenants* [D&C] 124 and RLDS D&C 107) dated 19 January 1841, which officially commanded the Saints to build the temple in Nauvoo. Daniel H. Wells, then a non-Mormon, donated the temple block to the Church. The actual construction commenced 8 March 1841. The structure was built with gray limestone from a quarry established at the north end of Main Street and with wood from a Wisconsin pinery. The temple measured 128 feet in length, 88 feet in width and 60 feet above ground to the overhang. A belfry and clock tower dome with a gilded angel weather vane was 158.5 feet above ground level (the modern water tower just behind the temple site is 130 feet in height). The walls were from four to six feet thick. There were thirty pilasters on the outside walls. At the bottom of each pilaster stood a moon stone. At the top was a sunstone. The star stones were set above the sunstones. In the middle of the attic face was the gilt inscription, "The House of the Lord. Built by the Church of Jesus Christ of Latter Day Saints. Commenced April. 6, 1841. Holiness to the Lord." The cost to complete the temple is estimated at nearly $1,000,000. The temple was divided into three stories and included a basement.[2]

Much of the city's energy over a five-year period went into building the temple. Work on the building was sustained by donations of money and time. Two types of tithing existed in Nauvoo: one on the

---

*A circle (O) above the heading indicates a standing structure or marker; a square (□) indicates that the structure is open to the public; and an asterisk (*) indicates that there is no present standing structure. Also see maps.

Nauvoo Temple. Daguerreotype courtesy of Missouri Historical Society.

financial increase or earnings and one on an individual's time. Each member was expected to donate one out of every ten days to the building of the temple.

Zina Diantha Huntington Jacobs recorded the events of the laying of the final capstone on 24 May 1845:

> This memorable day the Sun arose clear in the east. The morning was serene and silent. The Sun and Moon were at about equal height in the horizon, as if to rejoice with the Saints in Praises to the most high. The Saints went (all that knew it) to the Temple at 6 in the morning. The twelve and the workman, some brethren, the band with the banner of liberty floating in the gentle breeze, the last stone was laid on the Temple with shouts of Hosannah to God and the Lamb, amen and joy filled every bosom and thanks to our God that had preserved us. President Brigham Young made some remarks very appropriate. This is the seventh day even on which God rested from all his works and the Jews still keep it. O may Israel in these last days keep all thy statutes. O Praise the Lord for all his goodness, yea his

mercies endureth forever. Exalt his holy name for he hath no end. He hath established his word upon the Earth no more to be thrown down. He will remember all his covenants to fulfil them in their times. O praise the Lord forever more, Amen.[3]

During the final period of construction, Church leaders became concerned the temple might be burned by anti-Mormons. Hosea Stout recorded in his diary on 16 September 1845:

I went from thence to the temple and there it was decided that there be a guard kept night and day around the Temple and that no stranger be allowed to come within the square of the Temple Lot, and also that there be 4 large lanterns made for the purpose and placed about 25 feet from each corner of the Temple to keep a light by night for the convenience of the guard.[4]

Remains of the Nauvoo Temple. Tintype courtesy of LDS Historical Department.

The intense physical and emotional stress caused by mob action, preparations for the exodus west, the completion of the temple, and the everyday concerns with survival during the 1840s were released in various ways. During the spiritually charged period of December 1844 and January 1845, the Saints took time to refresh their minds and bodies through social recreation in the temple. William Clayton recorded such experiences in Heber C. Kimball's journal for 30 January 1845 and 2 January 1846:

> Thursday, 30th [1845] . . . the labors of the day having been brought to a close at so early an hour [8:30 P.M.] it was thought proper to have a little season of recreation; accordingly, Brother Hans Hanson was invited to produce his violin. He did so, and played several lively airs; several excellent songs were sung, in which several of the brethren and sisters joined. The "Upper California" was sung by Erastus Snow, after which Sister Whitney, being invited by President Young stood up, and invoking the gift of tongues, sang one of the most beautiful songs in tongues that was ever heard. The interpretation was given by her husband, Bishop Whitney. . . . the exercises of the evening were closed by prayer by President Brigham Young.
>
> Friday, January 2 [1846] After the regular exercises and business of the day were over . . . we had some excellent instrumental and vocal music, several members of the band having been invited in by Elder Kimball, William Pitt, William Clayton, J. G. Hutchinson and James Smithers. They performed several very beautiful pieces of music, and at the request of President Joseph Young played a Fisher's hornpipe, upon which he broke the gravity of the scene by dancing by himself. President Young then invited some others to join him in the dance. . . . after a short time spent in dancing . . . [President Brigham Young] alluded to the privilege which we now have of meeting in this house, and said that we could worship God in the dance, as well as in other ways.[5]

Besides being used to house social events, the temple was in use for several types of meetings before it was completed or dedicated. Brigham Young dedicated the baptismal font in the basement on 8 November 1841. The font was used for the performance of baptisms for the dead (proxy baptisms) and baptisms for health.[6] The temple ordinances were given by Joseph Smith to the Holy Order, sometimes called the Anointed Quorum. Before the Saints left Nauvoo these ordinances were administered to an estimated fifty-five hundred Saints in the temple, beginning on 10 December 1845. The attic room had been dedicated by Brigham Young on 30 November 1845 in preparation for the temple work beginning a few days later.

A bell was placed in the temple tower soon after it was finished. Hosea Stout's journal indicates one of the unintended uses for the bell. During the tense period of September 1845, the Nauvoo police and Nauvoo Legion placed guards around the city to protect the Saints from an assault upon Nauvoo by armed mobs. Several guards were placed at strategic points around and in the city. These guards were to be stationed "till further orders — orders that at the tolling of the Temple Bell every man knows it as an alarm and repairs forthwith armed and equipped to the parade ground," reported Stout.[7]

A special night dedicatory service for the entire building was held in the temple on 30 April 1846. The following day a public service was held. Orson Hyde, one of the Twelve Apostles, presided over the dedication session and offered the prayer. On 9 October 1848 the temple was gutted by an arsonist's fire. Several walls were razed by a tornado on 27 May 1850. The temple stones were used in many buildings in Nauvoo, including the old Nauvoo Jail just behind the temple on the next block. The remaining wall was purposely leveled in 1865. There is a model reproduction of the temple on display at the site and at the Nauvoo Restoration Inc. visitor center.

Temple lot after the destruction of the temple. Photograph courtesy of Archives and Manuscripts, Harold B. Lee Library, B.Y.U.

*

## 2. THE AMOS DAVIS STORE AND HOTEL SITE

The Amos Davis store and hotel was built near the southeast corner of Mulholland and Wells streets. Nonextant two-story brick building. Notice in the photo the arched entrances which are typical of the Federal style.

Remains, Amos Davis Store. Photograph courtesy of LDS Historical Department.

### Historical Background

Amos Davis was born on 20 September 1813 at Hopkinton, Rockingham County, New Hampshire. He married Mary Jane Scott on 1 January 1837. Davis was baptized in April 1840. He moved to Nauvoo in 1836. The Davis store, which was also used as a guest hotel, was in operation when the Saints arrived in the area. Davis was endowed in the Nauvoo Temple on 2 January 1846.[8]

The following are transactions, between 1839-1842, from the account ledgers for the store:

1) O. Granger 50 lbs flour $2.00; 2) Mrs. H. White blue ointment 12¢; 3) Hiram Smith 1 pair boys shoes $1.31 1/4; 4) O. Granger 13 lbs. pork 93¢; 5) James Mulholland 15 lbs nails $1.87, 1 pair boots $4.00; 6) O.S. Hunter apples 12¢; 7) Samuel Bent 1 gumlock $1.50; 8) S. Rigdon 6 lbs sugar 75¢; 9) Mrs. Everett 18 yards calico $1.62 1/2; 10) Thomas Bety 1/2 dozen chickens 75¢; 11) V. Knight 1 axe $2.25, 3 molasses 56¢, pepper 25¢, paper $1.83, candle $3.72; 12) H. Smith 1 box Lees pills 25¢; 12) Ben Warington 6 lbs nails 75¢; 1 yard ribbon 37 1/2¢; 2 yards calico 78¢; 13) Newell Knight 1 broom 31¢, 1 bed chord 37¢; 14) Stoddard 4 yards ribbon $2.50, 1 pair combs 6 1/4; 15) H. Clark 6 5/8 butter $1.62, 2 doz. eggs 25¢, molasses 84 1/2¢; 16) Miles 1 saw 37 1/2¢; 17) John Lytle 1/2 lb. almonds 12¢, 1/2 lb. raisins 6 1/4¢.[9]

It has been reported that Orrin Porter Rockwell lived at the hotel for a period of time:

Rockwell left Independence, [he left his family there]. He, meanwhile, took up residence in the tavern-hotel of a captain in the Nauvoo Legion named Amos Davis. Davis' inn also provided a more convenient headquarters for Rockwell from which to operate his carriage taxi service. Some said he took the job only as a subterfuge for his true purpose — spying on newcomers to the city.[10]

*

# 3. THE ROBERT FOSTER HOME SITE

The Robert Foster home was built at the northeast corner of Mulholland and Bluff (Woodruff) streets. Nonextant three-story brick building in the Federal style. Notice in the photo the clipped roof.

## Historical Background

Robert D. Foster was born on 14 March 1811 at Braunston, Northampton, England. He married Sarah Phinney on 18 July 1837 in Medina County, Ohio. Foster was baptized in 1839. Foster was a realtor heavily involved in land speculation during the Nauvoo period. He was also appointed as a regent of the University of Nauvoo and a county magistrate for Hancock County, Illinois. Foster joined a dissident movement in Nauvoo led by William Law and was one of the principals involved in the writing and printing of their newspaper, the *Nauvoo Expositor*.

On 21 January 1844, the Prophet Joseph Smith recorded the following in his journal: "Sunday, January 21 — 1844 Preached in front of Dr. Foster's Mammoth Hotel to several thousand people — although weather was somewhat unpleasant — on sealing the hearts of the fathers to the children and the hearts of the children to the fathers."[11]

Robert Foster home. Photograph courtesy of LDS Historical Department.

*

## 4.  THE NAUVOO EXPOSITOR BUILDING SITE

The Nauvoo Expositor building was built on the north side of Mulholland between Bluff (Woodruff) and Page streets. Nonextant two-story brick building.

## Historical Background

The *Nauvoo Expositor* newspaper was published on 7 June 1844 by several prominent dissidents from the Church including William and Wilson Law, Robert D. and Charles A. Foster, Frances and Chauncey Higbee, and Charles Ivins. William Law claimed that he wanted to reform the Church from within, but having failed to do so, he decided to publish his accusations in an attempt to "save" the Church from the so-called false teachings and practices which had been introduced in Nauvoo by the prophet.

The exaggerated accounts did not break the unity of the Saints against their prophet as William Law expected. On 10 June 1844 the city council met and acting under a liberal interpretation of its charter declared the *Nauvoo Expositor* a public nuisance and ordered it destroyed. This led to a complaint being issued against city officials on the charge of riot. This charge led directly to the murders of Joseph Smith and his brother Hyrum. William Law, one of the publishers of the *Nauvoo Expositor*, claimed a loss of about one thousand dollars in the press and equipment. The prophet was willing to pay expenses. Even after his death, Edward Hunter gave a note to the Laws, Fosters, and Higbees in an attempt to assist in settling the claim.[12]

Joseph Smith's journal recorded the actions of the city council concerning the *Nauvoo Expositor*:

> Monday, June 10, 1844. In City Council from 10 to 1:20 P.M. and from 2:20 to 5:30 P.M. investigating the merits of the Nauvoo Expositor, Laws, Higbee, Fosters and Council passed an ordinance concerning Libels and for other purposes, also issued an order to me to destroy the Nauvoo Expositor establishment as a nuisance. I immediately ordered the marshall to destroy it without delay. At the same issued an order to Jonathan Dunham, acting Major Gen[eral] Nauvoo Legion to assist the Marshall with the Legion if called upon so to do. And about 8 o'clock the Marshall reported that he had removed the press, type, and printed papers and fixtures into the street and fired them.[13]

William Law's journal entry for 10 June 1844 records his reaction to the city council action against the press:

> I was told that our press would be destroyed, but I did not believe it. I could not even suspect men of being such fools, but to my utter astonishment tonight upon returning from Carthage to Nauvoo I found our press had actually been demolished by the Marshal J.P.

Nauvoo Expositor Building. Photograph courtesy of Archives and Manuscripts, Harold B. Lee Library, B.Y.U.

Green, by order of the Mayor (Jos. Smith) and the city Council. The Marshall had the office door broken open by sledges, the press & type carried out into the street and broken up, they piled the tables, desks, paper etc. on top of the press and burned them with fire.[14]

The *Nauvoo Expositor* incident incensed certain elements in the county. In a community southwest of Nauvoo, Thomas Sharp, the publisher of the *Warsaw Signal* newspaper, called for the arrest of the Nauvoo city mayor and city council. Sharp was by far the leading anti-Mormon in Hancock County during the 1840s. He began in 1841 to use the *Warsaw Signal* as an instrument against the hierarchical and theocratic community at Nauvoo and to arouse anti-Mormon sentiment in the county. His editorial in June stated:

War and extermination is inevitable! CITIZENS ARISE, ONE AND ALL!!! Can you *stand* by, and suffer such INFERNAL DEVILS! to rob men of their property and RIGHTS, without avenging them. We have no time for comment; every man will make his own. LET IT BE MADE WITH POWDER AND BALL!!![15]

Joseph Smith was eventually charged in connection with the action against the newspaper. Believing the incident would quickly blow over, Joseph, his brother Hyrum, and a few trusted friends initially fled to Montrose to the home of William Jordan on the night of 22 June 1844. Joseph felt that no action would be taken against the Saints, since he believed he was the real target. Eventually he and Hyrum decided to return to Nauvoo, and they, along with other Church and city officials, surrendered themselves in the county courthouse in Carthage with assurances of protection by state governor Thomas Ford. While being held for trial in the Carthage jail, Joseph and his brother Hyrum were killed by a mob on the afternoon of 27 June 1844.[16]

O

# 5. THE NAUVOO HISTORICAL SOCIETY BUILDING

The Nauvoo Historical Society building is on the south side of Mulholland between Page and Barnett streets. Extant two-story brick building.

### Historical Background

This building was purportedly built by a Mormon who sold it to Dr. John F. Weld. Dr. Weld, a non-Mormon, practiced surgery and obstetrics during and after the Mormon period in Nauvoo. The Nauvoo Historical Society has purchased the property for its office and library.

The following advertisement appeared in the Nauvoo *Wasp*:

Dr. J.F. Weld practitioner in medicine, surgery, and obstetrics. Returns his thanks to the citizens of Nauvoo and adjoining country for the liberal patronage heretofore extended to him and respectfully solicits a continuation of the same. From the experience and success he has had during six years practice in the various diseases prevalent with this country he hopes to be enabled, by as assiduous attention to business to give ample satisfaction to all those who may favor him with a call. Particular attention will be paid to all affections of the eye. Nauvoo, Hancock co. Ill. April 30, 1842.[17]

O

# 6.   THE JOSEPH AGNEW HOME

The Joseph Agnew home is at the northwest corner of Mulholland and Robinson streets. Extant one and a half-story brick home, with later additions.

Joseph Agnew home. Photograph courtesy of Harold Allen.

## Historical Background

This home is believed to have been built by a Mormon family from St. Louis, in 1844. The Grubb and Ritchie store was located here during the Mormon period. Joseph B. Agnew occupied this home after the Mormon exodus in 1846. The Nauvoo Temple was gutted by a fire set by an arsonist on 9 October 1848, but no one was ever charged for the crime. However, Agnew made a deathbed confession that he started the fire. He told this story shortly before his death in the fall of 1870:

The reason for our burning it [the temple] was that there were continual reports in circulation that the Mormons were coming back to Nauvoo and we were afraid that they might take it into their heads to do so, and as we had had all the trouble with them we wanted, Judge Sharp . . . Squire McCauley . . . and myself . . . , determined the destruction of their Temple and by so doing they would not be able to ever again try to come back. So on the afternoon of the night it was burned, in order to make arrangements, we three met on the prairie about five miles south of Fort Madison in Illinois . . . and we pledged ourselves to destroy the Temple if it cost our lives. So we journeyed towards Nauvoo on horse back and on the way tried to perfect some plan to work on.[18]

*

## 7. THE EAST GROVE SITE

The East Grove was on the east side of Robinson between Mulholland and Knight streets.

### Historical Background

The East Grove, along with the West Grove and the temple site, was used for public meetings during the Mormon period. At the time no building existed that was suitable for large gatherings. This grove was later called the old Public Green. Joseph Smith delivered two important discourses here on Sunday, 16 June 1844, just a few days before his assassination. Thomas Bullock recorded part of one of these sermons:

> When things that are great are passed over without even a thought, I want to see all in all its bearings and hug it to my bosom — I believe all that God ever revealed and I never heard of a man being damned for believing too much but they are damned for unbelieving.[19]

Sunday services in Nauvoo consisted of a general worship meeting, which children attended, and some private Sunday evening prayer meetings in individual homes. Historical records fail to inform us how often the sacrament (The Lord's Supper) was administered at these general meetings that were often held at outdoor groves near the temple site. As many as eight thousand people attended such meetings at the temple site or in the East and West Groves. When the weather did not suit such large gatherings, the Saints met in each other's homes. Singing, reading scriptures, preaching the gospel, and bearing testimonies were all a part of these smaller meetings. Contemporary records indicate that speaking in tongues was not an unusual experience in these intimate meetings. There were also special "prayer circles" and other meetings of the "Holy Order." These consisted of members who had received special priesthood washings, anointings, priesthood endowment keys, and sealings from the prophet.[20]

Other special meetings held in Nauvoo were the family blessing meetings. These often consisted of adopted family members and blood relatives. Journals and diaries indicate that the father of the family would generally speak and conclude with a father's blessing over his family. Hot bread and sweet wine were served at these meetings.

*

# 8.   THE CHARLES C. RICH HOME SITE

The Charles C. Rich home was built near the southwest corner of Robinson and Knight streets. Nonextant two-story brick home.

### Historical Background

Charles C. Rich was born on 21 August 1809 in Campbell County, Kentucky. He married Sarah D. Pea on 11 February 1838 at Far West, Missouri. Rich was baptized on 1 April 1832 in Tazewell County, Illinois. He moved to Nauvoo in the fall of 1839. He was appointed to the Nauvoo High Council on 6 October 1839 and held several positions including being a member of the Nauvoo City Council, a Nauvoo University Regent, and the Nauvoo Fire Warden. He became a member of the Nauvoo Stake Presidency on 30 March 1841. He was endowed in the Nauvoo Temple on 12 December 1845, and was ordained a member of the Twelve Apostles on 12 February 1849 in Salt Lake City, Utah.

Rich owned several lots in Nauvoo, including a 1.25 acre wooded lot where he had built a log house. He purchased this property in 1842 and built a home here. He moved his family to this location on 2 September 1844.

> It was a happy time for us to once more feel at home among the Saints of God, and to be where we could hear words of comfort

from the mouth of our Prophet Joseph Smith. For we were now where we could attend meetings every Sunday. Also where we could visit with our dear brothers and sisters who like ourselves had been driven and robbed. And they like us were glad of a resting place out of the reach of those that had sought our lives and the lives of our Prophet and all our leaders who had been delivered from prison by the hand of our Heavenly Father. We were truly a thankful and humble people.[21]

Charles C. Rich home. Photograph courtesy of Archives and Manuscripts, Harold B. Lee Library, B.Y.U.

# *
# 9. THE HOWARD CORAY HOME SITE

The Howard Coray home was built near the northwest corner of Young and Barnett streets. Nonextant single-story log cabin.

## Historical Background
Howard Coray was born in 1817 in the state of New York. He married Martha J. Knowlton on 7 February 1841 at Nauvoo, Illinois.

Traditionally identified as the Howard Coray home. Photograph courtesy of Nauvoo Historical Society.

Coray was baptized on 24 March 1840. Coray arrived in Nauvoo in April 1840, and shortly after his arrival became a clerk to the Prophet Joseph Smith. Coray was also assigned to compile the Church's history and to be a clerk in the general tithing office. He was endowed in the Nauvoo Temple on 24 December 1845.

Coray recorded an interesting experience when Hyrum Smith visited his home in Nauvoo:

> My wife had a peculiar dream . . . she desired me to accompany her to Bro. Hyrum Smith's for the purpose of getting him to interpret it. We went the next Sunday to see him; but having company, he was not at liberty to say much . . . the next Sunday we went; but found as many at his house as the Sunday previous. He said to us, come again the next Sunday . . . but in a day or so he called at our house, and invited us to take a ride with him in his buggy . . . he commenced rehearsing the revelation on Celestial marriage . . . this was on the 22 of July 1843. The dream was in harmony with the Revelation . . . while still in the buggy, Bro. Hyrum asked my wife, if she was willing to be sealed to me; after a moment's thought, she answered, yes. He then asked me, if I wished to be sealed. I replied in the affirmation . . . he performed the ceremony, then and there.[22]

\*
# 10. THE ORSON SPENCER HOME SITE

The Orson Spencer home was built near the northwest corner of Young and Page streets. Nonextant two-story brick home.

### Historical Background

Orson Spencer was born on 14 March 1802 at West Stockbridge, Berkshire County, Massachusetts. He married Catherine Curtis on 13 April 1830. Spencer was baptized in 1841. He served as a member of the City Council, was Chancellor of the University of Nauvoo, and was a member of the Industrial Committee. He was elected mayor of Nauvoo in 1845. He was endowed in the upper floor of Joseph Smith's General Store on 2 December 1843, and in the Nauvoo Temple on 11 December 1845.

The *Manuscript History of the Church* for Sunday 6 March 1842 states: "I [Joseph Smith] preached at Elder Orson Spencer's near the Temple."[23]

Orson Spencer home. Photograph courtesy of Nauvoo Historical Society.

O

# 11.   THE JAMES HENDRICKS HOME

The James Hendricks home is on the north side of Young between Page and Bluff (Woodruff) streets. Extant two-story brick home.

## Historical Background

James Hendricks was born on 23 June 1808 near Franklin, Simpson County, Kentucky. He married Drusilla Dorris on 31 May 1827. Hendricks was baptized in 1835. The Hendricks family moved to Nauvoo in 1840. He was endowed in the Nauvoo Temple on 30 December 1845.

Drusilla Hendricks recorded the following in her reminiscences:

> We still continued to keep boarders . . . we finished our house in 1842 . . . I paid a good deal of tithing by making gloves and mittens. I did washing for bread or molasses for my children. Flour was hard

Traditionally identified as the James Hendricks home. Photograph courtesy of the authors.

to get. The winter set in early November [1842] and was very hard. I had to buy wood. I only [had] corn meal for bread . . . My husband asked me to lay aside my work and have prayer . . . When I was through I felt like I had poured out my whole soul to [the Lord] and I knew that we should have something [to eat]. I had no doubts. [Soon thereafter a gentleman sold them some fresh pork on credit which was not due and payable for twelve months.] Who could not see the hand of the Lord in this miracle worked on natural principle.[24]

☐

## 12. THE RAYMOND CLARK HOME AND STORE

The Raymond Clark home and store is at the northwest corner of Bluff (Woodruff) and Knight streets. Extant two-story brick home. The home is typical of the Federal style. Notice the double chimney built into the end walls.

Raymond Clark home. Photograph courtesy of Nauvoo Historical Society.

### Historical Background

Raymond Clark was born on 20 February 1798 at Wells, Rutland County, Vermont. He married Louisa Gill on 16 September 1827 at Antwerp, New York. Clark was apparently baptized in 1836. The Clark family moved to Nauvoo in 1840. He bought this lot from Daniel H. Wells for $200 and completed this home and store in 1843. Clark was endowed in the Nauvoo Temple on 23 December 1845.

The Clark store was a frequently visited business as contemporary journals indicate. For example, we note the following from Heber C. Kimball's journal:

9 April 1845 went to Brother Clark's with my wife to trade.

29 April 1845 went [to] Clark's Store to get things for my son [and] left my wife at the store.

6 May 1845 In the morning Clark's Store with my wife and daughter.[25]

O

## 13.   THE PARLEY P. PRATT HOME AND STORE

The Parley P. Pratt home and store is at the southeast corner of Wells and Young streets. Extant two-story brick home with strong Federal style influence.

### Historical Background

Parley P. Pratt was born on 12 April 1807 in Burlington, Otsego County, New York. He married Thankful Halsey on 9 September 1827 at Canaan, New York. Pratt was baptized on 1 September 1830 at Fayette, New York. He was ordained a member of the original Twelve Apostles on 21 February 1835. He was endowed in the upper floor of Joseph Smith's General Store on 2 December 1843 and in the Nauvoo Temple on 10 December 1845.

The following *Nauvoo Neighbor* advertisement provides some idea of the supplies carried by the Pratt & Snow Store.

Parley P. Pratt home. Photograph courtesy of LDS Historical Department.

NEW GOODS, VERY CHEAP. PRATT & SNOW, corner of Young and Wells streets, one block north of the Temple, Nauvoo, have just received from Boston the largest supply of Dry Goods ever opened in this city, consisting principally of good staple articles for fall and winter, such as Broad-cloths, Satinettes, Flannels, Shirtages, Sheetings, Calicoes, Boots, Shoes, etc. etc, Cash wanted, and country produce bought and sold. As we intend selling goods very cheap, and as the principle of honer, justice and impartially, no one need ask for credit, nor waste breath in bantering on the price, as we have but one invariable price either for cash or barter. Nauvoo, Nov. 7, 1843.
DRY GOODS, PROVISIONS dis.
Good news—100 percent reduction on the necessaries of life.[26]

In Nauvoo stores like Pratt's several mediums of exchange were used during this period. They included Nauvoo City scrip, Nauvoo Legion scrip, Nauvoo Legion Association (Arsenal) scrip, Nauvoo Seventies Hall certificates, Nauvoo Music Association certificates, Nauvoo Seventies Library certificates, Institute Association certificates, Nauvoo Agricultural certificates, and Manufacturing Association certificates. These notes were usually accepted only in the immediate area of Nauvoo.[27] Much-needed capital and cash remained a major problem for Joseph Smith as he organized the Saints into a community.

*

# 14.  THE NAUVOO LEGION ARSENAL AND OFFICERS' BUILDING SITES

The Nauvoo Legion Arsenal and Officers' buildings were built on the south side of Young between Wells and Durphy streets. Nonextant buildings. Arsenal was remodeled masonry.

## Historical Background

The Nauvoo City Charter provided for the creation of the Nauvoo Legion as part of the state militia. The Legion was organized on 3 February 1841. Joseph Smith was commissioned by Governor Thomas Carlin on 10 March 1841 as the top military officer. The Nauvoo Legion became an army of about 3,000.[28] Church leaders were determined to provide the Saints with the necessary protection against persecution like that encountered in New York, Ohio, and Missouri, yet Joseph claimed that the militia was also available for Illinois State purposes. This close connection between the city government and the Church eventually caused concern among the non-Mormons in Hancock County.

After Joseph Smith's death, Brigham Young was commissioned by Governor Thomas Ford on 24 September 1844 to fill Joseph's position. Supplies and weapons for the Legion were stored in various places, including the Masonic Temple. This was the major reason building an arsenal was proposed as early as 1843. Just to the west of the Arsenal a building for the officers of the Legion was erected.

Concerning the Arsenal, Heber C. Kimball recorded the following in his diary:

> July 17, 1845, Thursday. Went to the Temple and Arsenal as the roof was put on. President B. Young, W. Richards, A. Lyman, G.A. Smith, O. Pratt [were present] 43 Teams came to draw lumber.[29]

The Saints in Nauvoo also organized a junior Nauvoo Legion, a military organization for young men of the community, something done by many other towns of this period. These young men often practiced precision marching and riding along with basic military maneuvers.

The Nauvoo Arsenal. Photograph courtesy of Harold Allen.

Nauvoo Legion Officers Quarters. Photograph courtesy of LDS Historical Department.

□
# 15.   THE WILLIAM WEEKS HOME
# AND OFFICE

The William Weeks home and office is on the north side of Young between Durphy and Partridge streets. Extant single-story brick home built after the Federal style with an arched doorway.

William Weeks home. Photograph courtesy of the authors.

## Historical Background

William Weeks was born on 11 April 1813 in Martha's Vineyard, Dukes County, Massachusetts. He married Caroline Matilda Allen on 11 June 1841 at Nauvoo, Illinois. Weeks was baptized in the southern states. After his arrival in Nauvoo he was appointed Temple Architect. Although Joseph Smith was responsible for the temple design and general supervision, Weeks drafted numerous sketches, drawings, and handled the day-to-day construction problems. He also designed the Nauvoo House, the Arsenal, and the Nauvoo Masonic Temple. He was endowed in the Nauvoo Temple on 12 December 1845.

Joseph Smith's *History* states:

I instructed him [William Weeks] in relation to the circular windows designed to light office in the dead work of the arch between stories. He said round windows in the broad side of a building were a violation of all the known rules of architecture and contended that they should be semi-circular—that the building was too low for round windows, I told him I would have the circles, if he had to make the temple ten feet higher than it was originally calculated; that one light at the center of each circular window would be sufficient to light the whole room; that once the whole building thus illuminated, the effect would be remarkably grand. "I wish you to carry out my designs. I have seen in vision the splendid appearance of that building illuminated, and will have it built according to the pattern shown me."[30]

*

# 16. THE WEST GROVE SITE

The West Grove was on the east side of Partridge between Young and Mulholland streets.

### Historical Background

The West Grove, located in a ravine immediately west of the temple site, was one of several outdoor meeting places. A speaker's platform was erected and several benches were brought to the area to accommodate those attending. When weather permitted, a Sunday meeting at 10:00 A.M. was held in the Grove.

Joseph Smith delivered many discourses here during the last three years of his life. There are at least one hundred and seventy-three known public discourses.[31] The Saints were often anxious to attend these meetings. A non-Mormon resident of Nauvoo, Charlotte Haven, wrote, "we had not proceeded far when a large horse-sled . . . stopped before us . . . [we] were borne along with the multitude that were thronging to hear their beloved leader. Such hurrying! one would have thought it was the last opportunity to hear him they would ever have, although we were two hours before the services were to commence."[32]

During the late summer and early fall of 1842 Joseph Smith went into hiding because of the threat of unlawful arrest. Public appearances were almost nonexistent, but Joseph did take the opportunity on 29 August 1842 to speak to the Saints at the Grove:

Near the close of Hyrum's remarks I went upon the Stand. I was rejoiced to look upon the Saints once more, whom I have not seen

The West Grove. Photograph courtesy of the authors.

for about three weeks. They also were rejoiced to see me, and we all rejoiced together. My sudden appearance on the Stand under the circumstances which surrounded us, caused great animation and cheerfulness in the Assembly. Some had supposed that I had gone to Washington, and some that I had gone to Europe, while some thought I was in the City; but whatever difference of opinion had prevailed on this point, we were now all filled with thanksgiving and rejoicing.[33]

*

# 17.   THE EDWARD HUNTER HOME SITE

The Edward Hunter home was built on the east side of Partridge between Young and Mulholland streets. Nonextant two-story brick home built after the Federal style.

### Historical Background
Edward Hunter was born on 22 June 1793 at Newton, Delaware County, Pennsylvania. He married Ann Stanley on 30 September 1830

Edward Hunter home. Photograph courtesy of Special Collections Department, University of Utah Libraries.

in Delaware County, Pennsylvania. Hunter was baptized on 8 October 1840 in Pennsylvania. He moved to Nauvoo in 1842, served on the Nauvoo City Council and was appointed Bishop of the Nauvoo Fifth Ward in 1844. He was endowed in the Nauvoo Temple on 15 December 1845.

Joseph Smith was in hiding in the fall of 1842 because of threats of unlawful arrest. On 6 September 1842 he was in hiding at the residence of Edward Hunter. While in seclusion there he wrote a second important epistle regarding baptism for the dead, published in the *Times and Seasons* on 1 October 1842. This letter was incorporated in the 1844 *Doctrine and Covenants* (LDS 128/RLDS 110). Hunter recorded in his diary the following information about this period:

> Brother Joseph was hid up in my house from his enemies from Missouri. During that time, Joseph revealed the last part of the [instruction regarding] baptism for our dead. I was present with William Clayton.[34]

The home was also used as a safe house by members of the Twelve after Joseph's death. Heber C. Kimball recorded one such incident in his journal under the date 12 May 1845:

> Went home at five O'clock. Told family that I had got to hide up with my Brethren to keep away from writs, as there were several out for us. Went to Edward Hunters, in company with B. Young and W. Richards with the history of the Church and hid up in this upper room. Went to rest at 12 O'clock.[35]

# Old Commerce Area

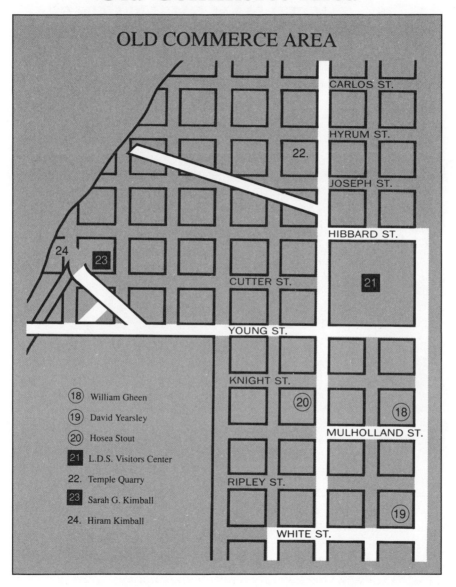

OLD COMMERCE AREA

18 William Gheen
19 David Yearsley
20 Hosea Stout
21 L.D.S. Visitors Center
22. Temple Quarry
23 Sarah G. Kimball
24. Hiram Kimball

O

# 18.   THE WILLIAM GHEEN HOME

The William Gheen home is on the west side of Partridge between Young and Mulholland streets. Extant two-story brick home, modified version of the Federal style.

William Gheen home. Photograph courtesy of RLDS Graphic Design Commission.

## Background Information

William A. Gheen was born on 2 September 1798 in Downington, Chester County, Pennsylvania. He married Ester Ann Pierre on 7 May 1823 at Concord, Pennsylvania. Gheen was baptized in August 1840. Gheen's daughter, Anna, married Heber C. Kimball. William and Ester Gheen were the great-grandparents of Spencer W. Kimball, twelfth president of the LDS Church. William Gheen died in Nauvoo on 12 July 1845. The sexton's weekly report in the *Nauvoo Neighbor*, dated 30 July 1845 announced Gheen's death of unknown causes.

Heber C. Kimball's journal indicates a close relationship with the Gheen family. On 23 August 1844, Kimball records: "In the afternoon [I] went Brother Gheen's with my [wife] Vilate. Several [others] present [I] blessed several."[36]

O

## 19. THE DAVID YEARSLEY HOME

The David Yearsley home is at the northwest corner of Partridge and White streets. Extant three-story brick home in the Federal style. Notice the glass transom over the door.

David Yearsley home. Photograph courtesy of LDS Historical Department.

### Historical Background

David D. Yearsley was born on 3 March 1808 at Thornbury, Chester County, Pennsylvania. He married Mary Ann Hoopes on 4 September 1830. Yearsley was baptized on 22 June 1841 in Nauvoo,

Illinois. He was a merchant and he operated two stores in Nauvoo. He was endowed in the Nauvoo Temple on 18 December 1845.

Mary Ann Yearsley remembered hers and her husband's baptisms, performed by the Prophet Joseph Smith at Nauvoo in the Mississippi River: "After the ordinance was performed, the Prophet swam out into the river a short distance, which greatly surprized the new members (and us) as they thought it a very strange thing for a Prophet to do."[37]

George A. Smith recorded his attendance at a gathering at the Yearsley home in 1845:

> Went to Brother David D. Yearsley's with my wife. The party consisted of about fifty. . . . Elders Orson Pratt, Willard Richards, John E. Page, John Taylor, Amasa Lyman, and their wives, besides Father and Mother, and many others composed the party. . . . Six widow Smiths were present, to wit: Aunt Lucy, widow of Joseph Smith, Sr., Mary the widow of Silas Smith; Mary the widow of Hyrum; Agnes, the widow of Don Carlos; Lavira, the widow of Samuel Harrison Smith, [Emma, widow of Joseph].[38]

## O
## 20.   THE HOSEA STOUT MARKER

The Hosea Stout marker is on the west side of Main between Mulholland and Young streets.

### Historical Background

Hosea Stout was born on 18 September 1819 at Danville, Mercer County, Kentucky. He married Samantha Peck on 1 January 1838. Stout was baptized in 1832. He was the captain of the Nauvoo police and was the clerk for the Nauvoo High Council. He lived in a home on the bluffs from 1844 to 1846 and was endowed in the Nauvoo Temple on 15 December 1845.

Extracts from Stout's journal record the following for 22 February 1845:

[J.P. Harmon and myself] went to the Lodge room [Masonic Hall] and locked ourselves up and talked over some particular matters relative to our eternal exaltation in the Kingdom of God and the absolute necessity of the brethren being united and maintaining our integrity to each other. We both were highly pleased with our interview and went on our way rejoicing. I then met with President Levi W. Hancock, who went with me to my house talking on the things of the Kingdom as with Brother Harmon. After we had eaten our dinner there we went down on the flat continuing the conversation as before, and parted and I went to the police and at dark went to the meeting of the Eleventh Quorum at the [Seventies] Hall as that was the time for the regular meeting of the Quorum at the Hall we had a good meeting. I delivered two short discourses and was followed by President Harmon Childs and others. Came home at 9 o'clock.[39]

During the summer of 1845, the Nauvoo Legion and police posted pickets on all roads leading into the city. Contingency plans were formulated in the event Nauvoo was attacked by anti-Mormon forces. Guards were also placed at key places in the city. Hosea Stout, chief of police in Nauvoo, spent most of his nights on guard duty at various locations throughout the city. He reported on 7 November that he "patrolled with other policemen till two, and then stood guard at Brother Brigham's till day, and came home about sunrise."[40]

☐

# 21. NAUVOO RESTORATION, INC. VISITOR CENTER (LDS CHURCH)

The Nauvoo Restoration Visitor Center is on the east side of Main between Young and Hibbard streets.

### Historical Background

Nauvoo Restoration, a non-profit organization sponsored by the LDS Church, began building this visitor center in May 1969. The building was dedicated on 4 September 1971. The Women's Monument Garden was dedicated in June 1978. The center offers introductory tours, including a movie released in 1989 entitled "Remembering

Nauvoo." It also has a research room in which patrons may identify property holdings as well as death and burial information concerning the early settlers of Nauvoo.

The LDS Church began buying historic sites and property in Illinois in 1905 when the county jail at Carthage was purchased. Beginning in 1937, small parcels of land, including parts of the Nauvoo Temple block, were acquired. Dr. James Leroy Kimball (a descendant of Heber C. Kimball, an early Nauvoo resident) purchased his great-grandfather's home in 1954. Dr. Kimball's restoration of this home to its 1840s appearance caused new interest in the historic section of the Nauvoo flats.

Dr. Kimball's vision of restoring part of old Nauvoo was facilitated by the creation of Nauvoo Restoration, Inc. in July 1962. The purpose of NRI is to "acquire, restore, protect, and preserve, for the education and benefit of its members and the public, all or a part of the old city of Nauvoo." Since that time NRI has purchased several homes, and it controls nearly 1,000 acres of land which Joseph Smith originally purchased to build the City of Nauvoo.[41]

*

# 22.   THE TEMPLE STONE QUARRY

The Temple stone quarry is on the west side of Main beyond the end of the asphalt street.

### Historical Background

The Temple stone quarry was operated by William Niswanger. Niswanger was born on 11 May 1796 at Middleton, Ferry County, Maryland. He married Mary Martin. The Niswangers had a child, Mary Jane, born in January 1843 in Nauvoo; but unfortunately the child died the following month. William was a member of the Nauvoo Legion and worked on the Nauvoo Temple. He was endowed in the Nauvoo Temple on 24 January 1846.

During the Mormon period, there were four stone quarries in and around Nauvoo, including the Hiram Kimball quarry, the Robert D.

Foster quarry, and the Temple stone quarry in Nauvoo proper. The Loomis quarry was located southeast of the city near the Mississippi River.

The Temple quarry was opened on 12 October 1840. Charles Drury and Albert Rockwood were placed in charge of the stonecutting for the Nauvoo Temple. The walls of the temple were made of solid blocks of cut limestone from four to six feet thick. The stones were rough cut and then transported to the temple site where they were dressed and polished. Many stones weighed up to two tons. Moses Horn was fatally wounded during the blasting at the quarry on 14 March 1845.

The following advertisement appeared in the *Nauvoo Neighbor*:

### LIME

To the Citizens of Nauvoo: The subscriber would respectfully inform the citizens of Nauvoo, and its vicinity, that he has commenced in burning LIME, and will keep on hand a constant supply during the present season, which he will sell cheaper than the cheapest. WM. NISWANGER. Nauvoo, June 17, 1843

N.B. All kinds of country Produce or Store Goods will be taken in exchange for lime, at his kilns, at the Temple Stone Quarry, on Main Street.[42]

An account from an "Old Nauvooer" tells of an incident that occurred near the Temple quarry:

It was Temple Tithing Day . . . [Brother Bybee] had hitched his team to his wagon and with his son had gone to the quarry to load a large stone into the wagon; then, they started for the temple. Pulling out of the quarry with its stone floor was no problem, but when they started across the "flat" their wagon became stuck in a mud hole. . . . [Brother Bybee] had just stepped off the wagon when [he saw] a man walking along the side of the street. . . . the man waded into the mud [to help dislodge the wagon] . . . the wagon moved a bit, and the horses were able to keep it going. After going about a hundred feet onto dry ground the boy let the team rest. . . . [Brother Bybee] called out, "Thank you, Brother Joseph." The boy was greatly impressed that a prophet of the Lord . . . was not above wading in mud halfway to his knees and getting his shoulder covered with mud to help another man in distress.[43]

☐
# 23.  THE SARAH GRANGER KIMBALL HOME

The Sarah Granger Kimball home is on the north side of Young beyond Bain street. Extant one and a half-story frame home, built during the pre–Mormon period. Notice the accentuated cornice over the door.

Sarah M. Granger home. Photograph courtesy of the authors.

## Historical Background

Sarah Granger Kimball was born on 29 December 1818 at Phelps, Ontario County, New York. She married Hiram S. Kimball on 23 September 1840 at Kirtland, Ohio. She was apparently baptized with her family before 1833. Her father's family moved to Commerce (Nauvoo), Illinois shortly after the Saints began gathering there. She was instrumental in founding the Nauvoo Female Relief Society. The preliminary meeting of the Relief Society was held at her home. She was endowed in the Nauvoo Temple on 20 January 1846.

Sarah Kimball recounts the story of the organization of the Relief Society:

In the spring of 1842, a maiden lady (Miss Cook) was seamstress for me, and the subject of combining our efforts for assisting the temple hands came up in conversation. She desired to be helpful, but had no means to furnish. I told her I would furnish material if she would make some shirts for the workmen. It was then suggested that some of the neighbors might wish to combine means and efforts with ours, and we decided to invite a few to come and consult with us on the subject of forming a Ladies Society. (The neighboring sisters met in my parlor and decided to organize. I was delegated to call on Sister Eliza R. Snow and ask her to write for us a constitution and by-laws and submit them to President Joseph Smith prior to our next Thursday meeting.) She cheerfully responded, and when she read them to him he replied that the constitution and by-laws were the best he had ever seen. "But," he said, "this is not what you want. Tell the sisters their offering is accepted of the Lord, and He has something better for them than a written constitution. Invite them all to meet me and a few of the brethren in the Masonic Hall over my store next Thursday afternoon, and I will organize the sisters under the priesthood after a pattern of the priesthood." He further said, "The Church was never perfectly organized until the women were thus organized."[44]

The women gathered together for the first official meeting of the Society on 17 March 1842. Several women—single and married, young and old—were organized to help administer relief to the poor and to sew clothing for those working on the temple. Emma Smith was chosen to preside over them. By 1844 more than 1,200 sisters had joined the organization. The Relief Society, unlike many of the women's benevolent societies of the day, went beyond the responsibilities of taking care of the poor in Nauvoo and contributed in various practical ways to building the temple.[45]

The involvement of women in diverse enterprises during the period was quite remarkable for the time. A few days following the organization of the Relief Society, Joseph Smith said that they "should move according to the ancient Priesthood, hence there should be a select . . . choice, virtuous and holy [Society]. [Joseph] said he was going to make of this Society a kingdom of priests as in Enoch's day—as in Paul's day."[46] In Nauvoo, Joseph Smith expanded the role of women in the Church through the introduction of temple worship and ritual. Women received these sacred ordinances and participated along with men— first in Joseph's Holy Anointed Quorum and later in the completed Nauvoo Temple.

*

# 24.  THE HIRAM KIMBALL STORE FOUNDATION

The Hiram Kimball store was built a short distance northwest of the Sarah Granger Kimball home. Nonextant single–story frame building.

Traditionally identified as the Hiram Kimball Store. Photograph courtesy of Archives and Manuscripts, Harold B. Lee Library, B.Y.U.

## Historical Background

Hiram Kimball was born on 31 May 1806 in West Farlee, Orange County, Vermont. He married Sarah M. Granger on 23 September 1840 at Kirtland, Ohio. Kimball was baptized on 20 July 1843 at Nauvoo, Illinois. He came to Commerce (Nauvoo) in 1833. He was extremely prosperous in Nauvoo and was engaged in numerous business activities during the Mormon period. Kimball was wounded in the Battle of Nauvoo, September 1846. He was endowed in the Nauvoo Temple on 17 January 1846.

The foundation of the store may be viewed by walking in a northwest direction behind the present day barn. The foundation is located about ten yards from the river bank. The above photograph has been often identified as the original store, more likely it was a barn on the Kimball property.

# Flats — East

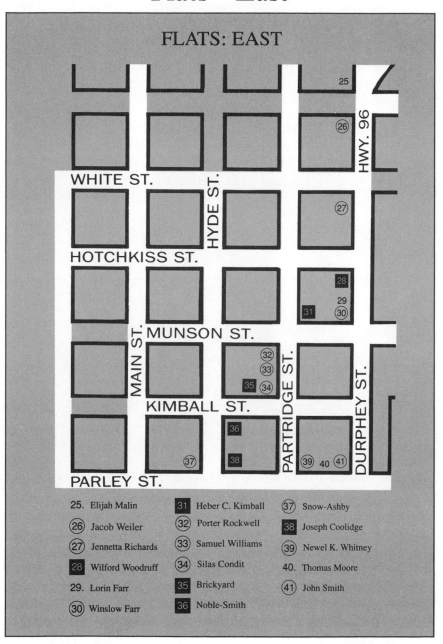

FLATS: EAST

25

26 HWY. 96

WHITE ST.

HYDE ST.

27

HOTCHKISS ST.

28
29
31 30

MAIN ST. MUNSON ST.

32
33
35 34
PARTRIDGE ST.

KIMBALL ST.

DURPHEY ST.

36

37 38 39 40 41

PARLEY ST.

25. Elijah Malin
26 Jacob Weiler
27 Jennetta Richards
28 Wilford Woodruff
29. Lorin Farr
30 Winslow Farr

31 Heber C. Kimball
32 Porter Rockwell
33 Samuel Williams
34 Silas Condit
35 Brickyard
36 Noble-Smith

37 Snow-Ashby
38 Joseph Coolidge
39 Newel K. Whitney
40. Thomas Moore
41 John Smith

*

## 25.   THE ELIJAH MALIN HOME SITE

The Elijah Malin home was built on the west side of Durphy (Highway 96) between Mulholland and White streets. Nonextant two-story brick home.

### Historical Background

Elijah Malin was born on 1 February 1774 at Willistown, Chester County, Pennsylvania. He married Catherine Essex on 19 March 1797 in Chester County, Pennsylvania. Malin was apparently baptized in 1840. He was endowed in the Nauvoo Temple on 18 December 1845.

Elijah Malin home (right) and Jacob Weiler home (left). Photograph courtesy of Harold Allen Collection.

O

## 26.   THE JACOB WEILER HOME

The Jacob Weiler home is on the west side of Durphy (Hwy 96) between Mulholland and White streets. Extant single-story brick home.

This home illustrates the simplicity of much of the early Nauvoo and other architecture of the period. Notice brick lintels over the door and windows.

### Historical Background

Jacob Weiler was born on 14 March 1808 in Churchtown, Lancaster County, Pennsylvania. He married Anna M. Malin on 12 August 1830 in Chester County, Pennsylvania. Weiler was baptized on 16 March 1840. The Weiler family arrived in Nauvoo on 6 July 1840. He was a contractor by trade and worked extensively on the temple. He was endowed in the Nauvoo Temple on 18 December 1845.

Jacob Weiler recalled that:

> After looking around for a few days [after their arrival in Nauvoo] I purchased a lot from the Prophet Joseph Smith in a very nice part of the city for which I paid eight hundred dollars. I afterwards built a nice brick home for my family. . . . We enjoyed our home in the city very much but our enemies were jealous of our happiness and prosperity and were determined we should not remain long unmolested . . . I crossed the river [June 1846] on a flat boat, having sold my house that cost me $1200 for $200.[47]

## O
## 27.  THE JENNETTA RICHARDS GRAVE MARKER

The Jennetta Richards grave marker is on the west side of Durphy (Hwy 96) between White and Hotchkiss streets.

### Historical Background

Jennetta Richards was born 21 August 1817 at Walkerfold, Lancashire, England. She married Willard Richards on 24 September 1838 in England. She was baptized on 31 July 1837 in England. She moved into her new home at Nauvoo on 21 November 1842. She was endowed in Joseph Smith's General Store on 1 November 1843.

She fell ill on 21 May and died on 9 July 1845. Willard, her husband, recorded:

Wednesday July 9, [1845] At day light dressed . . . [Jennetta] very weak. [I] kneeled, prayed, and laid hands on her three times . . . I gave her encouragement as I felt. She said, "how can I die under such progress?" About sunrise [I] sent for Levi [Richards] [and] about 6 [A.M.] sent for Elder H.C. Kimball, who came and laid on hands and prayed, she revived. [I] also sent for Father John Smith, John Taylor, [and] George A. Smith. Heber Kimball, John E. Page, Levi Richards, and myself dressed [in priesthood robes] prayed and went into her room anointed and prayed for her and felt encouraged. At fifteen minutes past 10 A.M. Jennetta stopped breathing . . . Sister Wilcox and Lucy Clayton watched and I slept in room on the floor.

Thursday July 10, 1845 Quorum meeting at my house. Sister Durphy, Sessions, Rhonda Ann, Lucy Clayton, and Sister Wilcox dressed Jennetta and put her in her coffin about sunset. Heber [Richards] said, "Pa, will you bury Ma in the garden, if you do I can bear it. If you do not I cannot bear it." I told him I would bury her in the garden.

Friday July 11, [1845] At dinner Rhonda Ann spoke out very pleasantly and said "Ma is gone away. She is gone to see Uncle Joseph and Hyrum and my little brother." I wept for joy to think of the happy meeting of Jennetta and Heber John. About sun set [we] laid the coffin in a pine box in a vault in the S.W. corner of the door yard. One foot east and north of the fence covering eight feet four inches long and four feet wide. Rhonda Ann called it the play house. Through a dahlia on the head of the coffin in the vault and said, "I will come and fetch it with her."[48]

☐
# 28.   THE WILFORD WOODRUFF HOME

The Wilford Woodruff home is at the southwest corner of Durphy (Hwy 96) and Hotchkiss streets. Extant two-story brick home. Notice the arched window in the attic space on the home's side elevation which is typical of the Federal style. Notice also the unusually large brick lintels over the windows.

## Historical Background
Wilford Woodruff was born on 1 March 1807 at Farmington, Hart-

ford County, Connecticut. He married Phoebe W. Carter on 13 April 1837 at Kirtland, Ohio. Woodruff was baptized on 31 December 1833 at Richland, New York. He was ordained a member of the Twelve Apostles on 16 April 1839. He moved to Nauvoo on 6 October 1841 and was elected to the Nauvoo City Council on 30 October 1841. He was endowed in the upper floor of Joseph Smith's General Store on 2 December 1843. Woodruff became the fourth president of the LDS Church on 7 April 1889 in Salt Lake City, Utah.

After his return to Nauvoo on 15 May 1843 from a missionary journey to England, he wrote:

> I have had for several days past some conversation with a number of the brethren concerning building a house for myself and family. As I had spent most of my time in the vineyard for the last ten years and would probably spend much of my time to come in the same way, I desired to have a house for my family to abide in and be comfortable in my absence. Several of the Brethren proffered to assist me to brick and other materials and help me put it into a house. Brother John

Wilford Woodruff home. Photograph courtesy of Archives and Manuscripts, Harold B. Lee Library, B.Y.U.

Fidoe would superintend the building. So, on this 22nd day of May we went onto the ground and staked out the ground for my house the dimensions of which are as follows laid out in Lot No 1 in Block 106 in the city of Nauvoo fronting Durphy Street on the east. It is to be 32 by 20 in the clear. Two stories high built of brick. I cleared away my ground and commenced digging my cellar for my house.[49]

Wilford Woodruff's journal documents the exodus from Nauvoo, which took several months. Even while Saints were moving across the river, others were just arriving from Great Britain or other missionary areas. The oddity of the situation is seen in his successive entries:

13th [April 1846]    We passed Quincy at 6 o'clock. We stopped at Warsaw. We also stopped at Keokuk for an hour. At about 2 o'clock we started to ascend the rapids. In about 2 hours we came in sight of the splendid Temple built by the Latter Day Saints and also the city of Nauvoo. I immediately got my spy glass and examined the city. The Temple truly looked splendid. We stopped at Montrose And then crossed to Nauvoo at the upper landing. I soon got a wagon & took my friends to my house where I had the happy privilege of meeting with my dear wife and children. I found them all well as could be expected.

14th    I had an interview with Br. Hyde and many Saints in Nauvoo. I found all the Saints struggling for life.

15th    In company with Father and Mother Woodruff and Phoebe's cousin Betsey Cossett, Sister Smoot and others we visited the Temple. We all went through each apartment of it from the font in the basement to the hall of the tower and had a view of all Nauvoo and the surrounding country. And after taking a view of each apartment of the Temple we again descended to the ground.

Within a few days Woodruff sold his home. He recorded in his journal: "I also sold my house and lot in which I [was] now living in for $675. I had a very busy day." On the following day he bought two wagons for $130. The next several days included preparations for the trip west. He continued his daily account:

17th    I spent the day in making some preparation to get away. . . . In the evening I commenced packing up my trunks once more for a long journey.

18th    I had a very busy day in packing up my things.

20th    It was a busy day. I am now preparing to get ready to start on the western journey. I have much to do and little time to do it in.

21st   Spent the day in running about to get my things ready.

22nd   There is considerable excitement concerning the mob making threats of coming upon Nauvoo to try to destroy the remainder of the Saints.

Wilford Woodruff, still preparing on 29 April: "[I finally finished] loading my wagons and took them over the river to Iowa. I took over two wagons, two yoke of oxen and two cows and sent Br. Ferguson to take care of the same." Later that evening "[I returned to Nauvoo and] repaired to the Temple and dressed in our priestly robes in company with Elder Orson Hyde and about 20 others of the Elders of Israel." During this busy period a few Church leaders remained in Nauvoo or returned from across the river to dedicate the temple in several public sessions.

We dedicated the Temple of the Lord built by the Church of Jesus Christ of Latter Day Saints, unto His Most Holy name. We had An interesting time. Notwithstanding the many false prophesies of Sidney Rigdon and others that the roof should not go on nor the House be finished and the threats of the mob that we should not dedicate it yet we have done both and we had an interesting time. At the close of the dedication we raised our voices in the united Shout of Hosanna to God and the Lamb which entered the Heavens to the joy and consolation of our hearts. We prayed for the Camp of Israel, for good weather, that we might not be disturbed by any mob until the dedication was over. I returned home thankful for the privilege of assisting in the dedication of the Temple of the Lord.

In the following days the "Saints began to gather at the temple at an early hour" to participate in several public dedicatory sessions. With the temple dedication completed, Woodruff started moving his family and provisions across the river to the camp of the Saints. The problems of such a move are described with honest weariness:

8th [May 1846]   I went over the river to the camp.

16   I crossed the Mississippi with my wagon and family to start on my journey to California. We camped about one mile from Montrose. I was very weary at night.

17th   Sunday This was one of the worst days of my life or most perplexing . . . As soon as we started the calves and cows all run various ways and while I was trying to get them together the oxen broke the tong out of my carriage. . . . Father drove into a mud hole and the oxen mired down. At last we finally got camped at black jack grove. And I was very weary at night. 4 miles.

21st   I spent the day in camp. We had a rainy night and many things wet.

On the following day Woodruff left the city for the last time and began his journey west with the Saints. He recorded with nostalgia his feelings as he viewed the city and temple:

I left Nauvoo for the last time perhaps in this life. I looked upon the Temple and City of Nauvoo as I retired from it and felt to ask the Lord to preserve it as a monument of the sacrifice of his Saints. I returned to the camp and spent the night 10 miles.[50]

*

## 29.   THE LORIN FARR HOME SITE

The Lorin Farr home was built on the west side of Durphy (Hwy 96) between Hotchkiss and Munson streets. Nonextant single-story brick home.

Lorin Farr home. Photograph courtesy of Special Collections Dept., University of Utah Libraries.

## Historical Background

Lorin Farr was born on 27 July 1820 at Waterford, Caledonia County, Vermont. He married Nancy B. Chase on 1 January 1845 at Nauvoo, Illinois. Farr was baptized on 19 May 1832 in Clyde, Vermont. He moved to Nauvoo in the spring of 1840. Lorin was the son of Winslow Farr who had completed a brick home next door the previous year. Lorin had a small dwelling, and was a tenant on this lot from 1845–1846. He was endowed in the Nauvoo Temple on 16 December 1845.

Lorin Farr recorded one of his activities in Nauvoo during this period:

> A number of young people assembled at the house of Elder H.C. Kimball, who warned them against the various temptations to which youth are exposed . . . another meeting was held in the ensuing week at [my] school-room, which was filled to overflowing. Elder Kimball delivered addresses, exhorting young people to study the scriptures . . . the next meeting was appointed to be held at my house . . . it was completely filled at an early hour. Elder Kimball, as usual, delivered an address. . . . My house being too small, the next meeting was appointed to be held in the hall over my store. I addressed the young people for some time.[51]

Nauvoo was not only a city of adult men and women, but also a city of children and young adults. The city charter provided a comprehensive common school system. There is evidence of many teachers in Nauvoo during the period, often in each ward. Nauvoo also included a seminary (high school) and a university. Adults had other opportunities for learning as well—for example, through the Nauvoo Library and Literary Institute. A unique feature of these schools was that anyone wishing an education could attend; the system was financed through public taxation.

## O
## 30.   THE WINSLOW FARR HOME

The Winslow Farr home is at the northwest corner of Durphy (Hwy 96) and Munson streets. Extant two-story brick duplex home.

Winslow Farr home (mislabeled). Photograph courtesy of LDS Historical Department.

## Historical Background

Winslow Farr was born on 12 January 1794 at Chesterfield, Cheshire County, New Hampshire. He married Olive H. Freeman on 5 December 1816 at Waterford, Vermont. Farr was baptized on 19 May 1832. The Farr family moved to Nauvoo in the Spring of 1840. He was endowed in the Nauvoo Temple on 15 December 1845.

This duplex has been referred to as the Aaron and Lorin Farr homes. Winslow Farr was the father of Aaron and Lorin, which may explain the confusion. While all three may have been involved in building this home and may have lived there briefly, the lot was owned by Winslow Farr from 1843–1846.

☐
# 31. THE HEBER C. KIMBALL HOME

The Heber C. Kimball home is at the northeast corner of Munson and Partridge streets. Extant two-story brick home with both Federal and Greek Revival features. The main two-story structure was erected in 1845, while the one and a half-story addition dates from the post-Mormon period. An inscription stone above the balcony reads H.C.K. 1845.

## Historical Background

Heber C. Kimball was born on 14 June 1801 at Sheldon, Franklin County, Vermont. He married Vilate Murry on 7 November 1822 near Mendon, New York. Kimball was baptized on 16 April 1832 at Mendon, New York. He was ordained as an original member of the Twelve Apostles on 14 February 1835. In 1841 he traded a piece of property for this lot. Kimball originally built a log house with three lower rooms and one upstairs, and later built this brick structure. Under the direction of Heber C. Kimball, a Young Gentlemen's and Young

Heber C. Kimball home. Photograph courtesy of LDS Historical Department.

Ladies Relief Society of Nauvoo was organized for Nauvoo's young men and women. He was endowed in the upper floor of Joseph Smith's General Store on 4 May 1842, and again in the Nauvoo Temple on 10 December 1845. Kimball was a member of the LDS Church First Presidency with Brigham Young at Salt Lake City, Utah.

The following from Kimball's journal briefly describes some work on his home in Nauvoo:

> July 4, 1845, Friday—Had six masons come to work and four tenders. The day pleasant. Brothers Wallis and Solen Foster come and put the joists on the 2 floors of my house. Many of the Saints spent the day riding and music, and in different ways to amuse themselves. The Divernon come up from St. Louis, Quincy and other places for pleasure. Stopped in our city they went all over the city. Very civil. All things passed well and the Lord was with us.[52]

O

# 32.   THE PORTER ROCKWELL MARKER

The Porter Rockwell marker is at the southwest corner of Munson and Partridge streets.

### Historical Background

Orrin Porter Rockwell was born on 28 June 1813 at Belcher, Hampshire County, Massachusetts. He married Luana Beebe on 2 February 1832 in Jackson County, Missouri. Rockwell was baptized on 6 April 1830 at Fayette, New York. In Nauvoo, Rockwell served as a personal bodyguard to Joseph Smith. He was endowed in the Nauvoo Temple on 5 January 1846.

O

# 33.   THE SAMUEL WILLIAMS HOME

The Samuel Williams home is on the west side of Partridge between Munson and Kimball streets. Extant two-story brick home with post–Mormon addition.

Samuel Williams home. Photograph courtesy of LDS Historical Department.

### Historical Background

Samuel Williams was born 22 March 1789 at Russell, Hampden County, Massachusetts. He married Ruth Bishop on 19 March 1810 at Westfield, Massachusetts. Williams was baptized in 1839. He was appointed to preside over the elders' quorum in Nauvoo in 1841. Williams worked as a stonecutter on the Nauvoo Temple. He was endowed in the Nauvoo Temple on 15 December 1845.

○

# 34.   THE SILAS CONDIT HOME

The Silas Condit home is at the northwest corner of Partridge and Kimball streets. Extant two-story brick home with later additions.

### Historical Background

Silas W. Condit was born on 27 June 1819 at Newark, Essex County, New Jersey. He married Julia Ann Parker on 13 February 1842 in Delaware County, Ohio. Condit was baptized on 3 February 1842. He was endowed in the Nauvoo Temple on 7 January 1846.

Silas Condit home. Photograph courtesy of LDS Historical Department.

□

# 35.   THE BRICKYARD

The brickyard is on the north side of Kimball between Partridge and Hyde streets.

## Historical Background

There were numerous brickyards in Nauvoo during the Mormon period, including the Colton brickyard near Hibbard and Rich streets; the Clark & Webster yard on Parley Street; the Nauvoo brickyard on Young Street; and the Mathews yard at his residence about two miles northeast of the temple. Since brick buildings were rapidly replacing the wooden and log structures in Nauvoo, a large supply of bricks was needed. For example, the Noble-Smith home contains over 30,000 bricks. On the first floor the walls are three bricks thick while the second floor walls are two bricks thick.

The clay for the bricks came from upper Nauvoo. It was formed into bricks and then heated in a kiln to 2100 degrees. It took about twenty-one days for a brick to dry after firing. Every other day the bricks had to be turned to allow them to dry uniformly. The production of bricks became an extremely important part of the economic and social aspects of Nauvoo. Brick production and brick masonry employed hundreds. The spacious and more permanent homes and buildings provided for larger gatherings of all kinds.

☐

# 36. THE NOBLE-SMITH HOME

The Noble-Smith home is near the southeast corner of Kimball and Hyde streets. Extant two-story brick home.

## Historical Background

Joseph B. Noble, the original owner, was born in Massachusetts in 1810. He married Mary A. Beman in 1834. Noble was baptized in 1832. He acquired the lot for the present house in 1841 and erected this home in 1843. When the Saints left Nauvoo in 1846, the Church trustees arranged with Noble to transfer the home to Lucy Mack Smith, the prophet's widowed mother. Noble was endowed in the Nauvoo Temple on 15 December 1845.

Lucy Mack Smith was born on 8 July 1775 at Gilsum, Cheshire County, New Hampshire. She married Joseph Smith Sr. on 24 January 1796 at Tunbridge, Vermont. Lucy was baptized on 6 April 1830 at Fayette, New York. After arriving in Nauvoo, she and her husband

Noble-Smith home. Photograph courtesy of LDS Historical Department.

lived in a log cabin on the Joseph Smith homestead property. Later they moved to a new home on the southeast corner of Main and Water streets. She then moved into this home after the general exodus in 1846. She was endowed on or before 8 October 1843 in the upper floor of Joseph Smith's Mansion House and in the Nauvoo Temple on 11 December 1845.

□
## 37.   THE SNOW-ASHBY DUPLEX

The Snow-Ashby duplex is near the northwest corner of Hyde and Parley streets. Extant two-story brick duplex home with Greek Revival doors and double windows.

### Historical Background

Erastus F. Snow was born on 9 November 1818 at St. Johnsbury, Caledonia County, Vermont. He married Artemesia Beaman on 3 December 1838. Snow was baptized on 3 February 1833. In 1843 he

Snow–Ashby Duplex. Photograph courtesy of Harold Allen.

arranged to have a house built on a lot his wife had inherited from her father's estate. He then sold half of the property to Nathaniel Ashby, whom Snow had converted on a proselytizing mission, and had the contract for the house doubled. He was endowed in the Nauvoo Temple on 12 December 1845. Erastus Snow was ordained a member of the Quorum of the Twelve Apostles on 12 February 1849 in Utah.

Nathaniel Ashby was born on 15 April 1805 at Salem, Essex County, Massachusetts. He married Susan Hammond on 30 November 1826 at Salem, Massachusetts. Ashby was baptized on 12 December 1841, and moved to Nauvoo in 1843. He was endowed in the Nauvoo Temple on 30 December 1845.

Erastus Snow recorded in his journal his final days in Nauvoo:

> I effected a sale of as much of my household stuff and personal property as possible at a great sacrifice, and gathered up what teams and provisions I could and started on the 16th of February, leaving my buildings and real estate to the amount of Two Thousand Dollars (as did also the rest of the company) at the disposal of Brothers Babbitt, Heywood, and Fullmer, the new trustees elected to remain and complete the lower stories of the Temple, attend to the sale of property, and wind up the affairs of the Church in Nauvoo, and from the proceeds of such sales to assist the poor in following us.[53]

☐
## 38.   THE JOSEPH COOLIDGE HOME
## AND WORKSHOP

The Joseph Coolidge home and workshop is at the northeast corner of Hyde and Parley streets. Extant two-story frame home. Notice the New England influence in the triple windows.

Joseph W. Coolidge home. Photograph courtesy of LDS Historical Department.

### Historical Background
Joseph W. Coolidge was born on 31 May 1814 at Bangor, Penobscot County, Maine. He married Elizabeth Buchannan on 12 December 1834. Coolidge was baptized before 1838. In 1843, he built this two-story frame house, which he used as a residence and workshop. Coolidge was a member of the Nauvoo City Council and the administrator of the Joseph Smith estate. He was endowed in the Nauvoo Temple on 16 December 1845.

On the west gable is an inscription placed on the home by a Mr. Kaufman after the Mormon exodus. He placed the date of the building of the home, his name, and an inscription in German that means:

"This house is mine and yet not mine. Who comes after me shall find the same. I have been here and who reads this shall also have been here." This German adage seems to imply a sense of hospitality.

Coolidge advertised in the *Nauvoo Neighbor*:

> The subscriber, having purchased a quantity of seasoned lumber, all kept constantly on hand and made to order all kinds of window sash and doors and all kinds of job work in their line of business, at the shortest notice for city or country produce. Shop on the corner of Parley and Carlin streets. JOSEPH W. COOLIDGE & CO.
>
> N.B. Those having accounts against the above firm for work or materials will please bring them in immediately for settlement. J.W.C. & CO.[54]

O

## 39. THE NEWEL K. WHITNEY HOME

The Newel K. Whitney home is at the northeast corner of Parley and Partridge streets. Extant two-story brick home with post-Mormon period additions.

### Historical Background

Newel K. Whitney was born on 5 February 1795 at Marlborough, Windham County, Vermont. He married Elizabeth A. Smith on 20 October 1822. Whitney was baptized in November 1830 at Kirtland, Ohio. He settled in Nauvoo in 1839. He was appointed Bishop of the Nauvoo Middle Ward shortly after his arrival in Nauvoo and was elected alderman for the city on 1 February 1841. He was endowed in the upper floor of Joseph Smith's General Store on 4 May 1842, and in the Nauvoo Temple on 10 December 1845.

Three men appeared at Joseph Smith's home undetected in August 1842 in an attempt to arrest him:

> When they arrived, President Joseph Smith was in another apartment of the house, eating dinner with his family. John Boynton happened to be the first person discovered by the sheriffs, and they began to ask him where Mr. Smith was. . . . While this conversation was going on, President Joseph Smith passed out the back door, and through the corn in his garden to Brother Newel K. Whitney's. He went up stairs undiscovered.[55]

Traditionally identified as the Newell K. Whitney home. Photograph courtesy of Harold Allen.

*

# 40.   THE THOMAS MOORE HOME SITE

The Thomas Moore home was built on the north side of Parley between Partridge and Durphy (Hwy 96) streets. Nonextant two-story brick home and limestone building.

### Historical Background

Thomas Moore was born 15 June 1801 aboard a ship on the Atlantic Ocean somewhere between Belfast, Ireland and New York City. He married Mahala D. Higby in approximately 1825. Moore was probably baptized in 1842. He was endowed in the Nauvoo Temple on 16 December 1845.

Thomas Moore home. Photograph courtesy of LDS Historical Department.

O

## 41. THE JOHN SMITH HOME

The John Smith home is near the northwest corner of Parley and Durphy (Hwy 96) streets. Extant two-story brick home, typical salt-box style.

### Historical Background

John Smith was born on 16 July 1781 at Derryfield, Rockingham County, New Hampshire. He married Clarissa Lyman on 11 September 1815. Smith was baptized on 9 January 1832. He moved to Commerce (Nauvoo), Illinois in 1839. Over the next five years he was the presiding Church authority in Lee County, Iowa and in Ramus, Illinois. He returned to Nauvoo in August 1844 and was thereafter appointed president of the Nauvoo Stake. He was endowed in the upper floor of Joseph Smith's General Store on 28 September 1843, and in the Nauvoo Temple on 10 December 1845. Smith was later ordained the LDS Church Patriarch on 1 January 1849 in Salt Lake City, Utah.

During the Church's general conference held in October 1839, it was decided that a stake (an administrative jurisdiction unit) should be organized at Commerce. The new stake was a gathering place for the members of the Church and consisted of three wards (city administrative sections). In addition to the use of wards as political administrative divisions, the Mormons used them for ecclesiastical purposes in Nauvoo, with a Church leader (bishop) designated for each ward. In March 1840, the city was divided into four wards, and on 20 August 1842 into ten wards. This reflected the growth of the city as many Saints arrived from Britain and other parts of North America.

John Smith made the following observation in his diary on 8 February 1846:

> After making every preparation to our power, with our scanty means, agreeable to the counsel of the Church, we collected our family, consisting of myself and wife and sister Brimhall to do our cooking on the road; John Lyman Smith, who had been married a few months previous to Augusta B., daughter of John and Sarah M. Cleveland; Caroline, who was married to Thomas Callister. We commenced crossing the river, the weather being very cold and with large quantities of ice running in the river. We leave in the City of Nauvoo a good house of brick and a quantity of good furniture, without making a sale of anything.[56]

John Smith home. Photograph courtesy of Nauvoo Historical Society.

# Nauvoo State Park Area

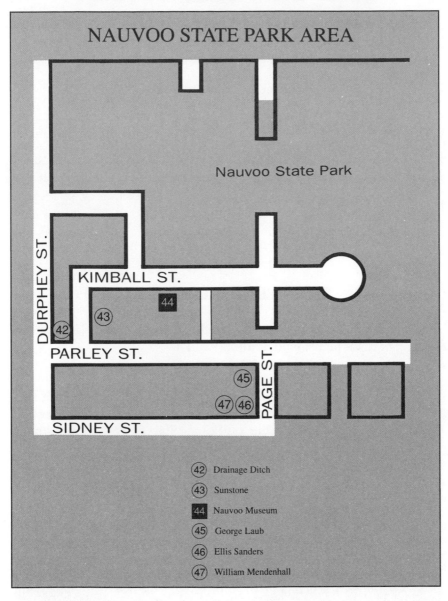

NAUVOO STATE PARK AREA

Nauvoo State Park

DURPHEY ST.

KIMBALL ST.

44

43

42

PARLEY ST.

PAGE ST.

45

47 46

SIDNEY ST.

42 Drainage Ditch

43 Sunstone

44 Nauvoo Museum

45 George Laub

46 Ellis Sanders

47 William Mendenhall

O

# 42.   THE DRAINAGE DITCH

The drainage ditch is along the east side of Durphy (Hwy 96) street.

### Historical Background

This ditch was created to catch the rapid runoff of water from upper Nauvoo that would settle in the flats. The soil in this area has a high clay content and the limestone level is close to the surface. The clay and limestone prevented the water from being absorbed into the water table, producing the marshy flats until the drainage ditch was completed.

O

# 43.   THE TEMPLE SUNSTONE

The temple sunstone is on the north side of Parley in the Nauvoo State Park. (See also the Nauvoo Temple, no. 1.)

### Historical Background

The Nauvoo Temple construction called for the inclusion of several symbolic features, including a baptismal font on the back of twelve oxen in the basement of the building. Star stones, moon stones, sunstones, and a weather vane in the form of an angel were also used. Three sunstones are known to still exist: one is located in Nauvoo, another is owned by the RLDS Church, and the third is in the Smithsonian Institute in Washington D.C. Two moon stones are on display at the Joseph Smith Homestead and another at the Hotel Nauvoo on Mulholland Street. A star stone may be seen in the Seventies Hall Museum on Parley Street.

The baptismal font was first constructed of wood, but later the twelve oxen were replaced with stone oxen. The Old Testament mentions a "laver" in the Temple of Solomon which was placed on the back of twelve oxen (see 1 Kings 6). The twelve oxen may represent the twelve tribes of Israel. The Nauvoo Temple's baptismal font was

placed underground in the basement which could represent the resurrection, as baptism is symbolic of death and rebirth (see Romans 6 and
Colossians 2).

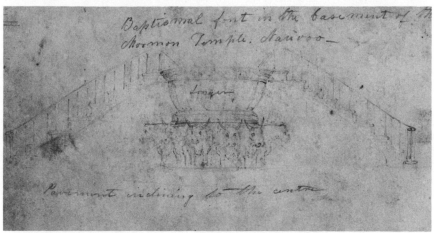

Drawing for Baptismal Font, Nauvoo Temple. Photograph courtesy of Missouri
Historical Society.

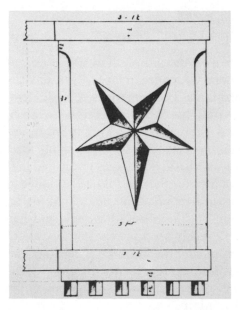

Nauvoo Temple Star Stone. Drawing by
William Weeks (architect of Nauvoo
Temple) courtesy of Harold Allen.

Nauvoo Temple Sunstone. Photograph courtesy of Archives and Manuscripts, Harold B. Lee Library, B.Y.U.

The star stones on the temple had five points. The moon stones were crescent moons with human faces (eyes, mouths, and noses). The sunstones also had faces. The sunstones were 2.5 feet broad, and ornamented with rays of lights. Above these rays were two hands holding trumpets.[57] On 16 February 1832 Joseph Smith and Sidney Rigdon received several important visions concerning life after death. This revelation, known as "the Vision," was published in the Church newspaper, *Evening and Morning Star*, in July 1832. Later, the revelation was incorporated into the 1835 *Doctrine and Covenants* Section 91 (current LDS D&C section 76). Joseph and Sidney said heaven consisted of three levels. These levels are known as the Celestial Kingdom, the Terrestrial Kingdom, and the Telestial Kingdom, each represented by a heavenly object. The sun represents the glory of the Celestial world, the moon the glory of the Terrestrial Kingdom, and the stars the glory of the Telestial Kingdom.

A drawing of the Nauvoo Temple weather vane is found in the LDS Church Historical Department. It was placed on the temple on

Nauvoo Temple Moon stone. Photograph courtesy of RLDS Graphic Design Commission.

30 January 1846 and was described by Perrigrine Sessions in his journal in 1846:

> On this day [30 January 1846] they raised the vane which is the representation of an angel in his priestly robes with a book of Mormon in one hand and a trumpet in the other which is over laid with gold leaf.[58]

The angel is also wearing a cap on his head and above him are a square and compass. During the last few months of Joseph's life, he spoke frequently to the Saints regarding the temple and the blessings promised to the faithful. In these discourses, given between April and June 1844, the prophet quoted extensively from the Book of Revelation. Joseph saw strong connections between the symbolism of Revelation and temple worship. For example, Revelation 14 speaks of "another angel flying in the midst of heaven having the everlasting gospel to preach to them that dwell on the earth, and to every nation, and kindred, and tongue, and people." From the Church's inception,

Nauvoo Temple Weather Vane. Drawing courtesy of Dane Calkins.

Nauvoo Temple Bell. Photograph courtesy of Utah State Historical Society.

the Saints have identified this messenger as the Angel Moroni, who first appeared to the prophet in September 1823. Moroni's flowing robes, mentioned above, might represent the priestly robes Sessions describes. The cap could be symbolic of crowns, as mentioned in Revelation. The Saints are kings and priests of God (Rev. 1:6). The robes, therefore, may be symbolic of the priesthood, while the crowns possibly represent royalty. For Joseph Smith, the ordinances of the temple gave men a fullness of the priesthood, which was to be a king and a priest to God.[59]

Josiah Quincy, a later mayor of Boston, visited the prophet in Nauvoo in 1844, and recorded the following:

> Near the entrance to the Temple we passed a workman who was laboring upon a huge sun, which he had chiselled from the solid rock. . . . "General Smith," said the man, looking up from his task, "is this like the face you saw in vision?" "Very near it," answered the Prophet, (this was added with an air of careful connoisseurship that was quite over-powerful) "except that the nose is just a thought too broad."[60]

O

# 44. THE NAUVOO HISTORICAL SOCIETY MUSEUM

The Nauvoo Historical Society Museum is on the south side of Kimball in the Nauvoo State Park. Extant two-story brick home. The post-Mormon period additions include a wine cellar.

## Historical Background

This structure is a Mormon period home believed to have been built by the Wagner family. It is also known as the Rheinberger home because it was the residence of that family after the exodus in 1846.

The National Park Service, Illinois State Historical Society, and many private individuals have supported and contributed to the success of restoring Nauvoo to its 1840s state. The state of Illinois designated certain areas in Nauvoo as a part of the State Parkway in 1936. An important part of the restoration of Nauvoo was the designation of

Nauvoo Historical Society Museum. Photograph courtesy of LDS Historical Department.

the city as a National Historical Site by the National Park Service in 1961.

The state park in Nauvoo and the Nauvoo Historical Society Museum are dedicated to preserving Nauvoo's past by acknowledging the contributions of the Indians, white settlers, Mormons, Icarians, Germans, Swiss, and current residents.

O

## 45.   THE GEORGE LAUB HOME

The George Laub home is on the south side of Parley near Page Street. Extant two-story brick home built in the Federal style. Notice the iron stars that are used to hold rods in the structure and that help stabilize the walls.

### Historical Background
George Laub was born 5 October 1814 at Earl, Lancaster County,

George Laub home. Photograph courtesy of the authors.

Pennsylvania. He was married to Mary J. McGinness on 6 January 1846 at Nauvoo, Illinois. Laub was baptized on 12 March 1842. He moved to Nauvoo shortly after his conversion. In Nauvoo he worked as a joiner, working forty days in the temple stone quarry in lieu of paying tithing. He was a member of the Nauvoo Library and Literary Institute. He was endowed in the Nauvoo Temple on 19 December 1845.

Laub's journal indicates the trouble the Saints had with anti-Mormons during the critical winter of 1845–46:

> Now I told Brother Megenness [a friend of the family] that he better move to my house in the city. So he got Brother Roberts to haul the best of his goods that night to the city. Also Brother Russell came to our assistance and we labored all that night. So we moved to the city of Nauvoo, as we then lived four miles east of the city. Now Brother Megenness crossed with part of his family and we sold his farm at less than the house cost him. Now by this time the mob grew bolder and was all round the city and our lives were in danger.[61]

○

# 46. THE ELLIS SANDERS HOME

The Ellis Sanders home is at the northwest corner of Page and Sidney streets. Extant two-story brick home in the typical Federal style with post–Mormon additions.

## Historical Background

Ellis M. Sanders was born on 5 December 1808 in Stanton, New Castle County, Delaware. He married Rachel B. Roberts on 9 November 1839. Sanders was baptized on 18 September 1843. He was endowed in the Nauvoo Temple on 18 December 1845.

Ellis Sanders signed an agreement with William and James Mendenhall to have this home built.

> Be it remembered that on this fifteenth day of May, in the year of our Lord one thousand eight hundred and forty-four William and James Mendenhall . . . covenant with said Ellis M. Sanders . . . will within

Ellis Sanders home. Photograph courtesy of the authors.

the space of nine months, in good and workman like manner and at their proper charge and expense, at the city of Nauvoo, county of Hancock and State of Illinois, will and substantially erect, build, and finish one brick House.[62]

○

# 47.  THE WILLIAM MENDENHALL HOME

The William Mendenhall home is on the north side of Sidney near Page Street. Extant two-story brick home with minimal architectural definition.

### Historical Background

William Mendenhall was born on 8 April 1815 at Mill Creek Hundred, Newcastle County, Delaware. He married Sarah Lovell on 21

William Mendenhall home. Photograph courtesy of Mendenhall family.

February 1838. Mendenhall was baptized on 12 December 1841. He arrived at Nauvoo for a visit on 30 May 1842. He stayed at the Mills or City Hotel at the northwest corner of Main and Sidney streets. He worked as a woodcutter and brick mason while in Nauvoo. He also worked on the Nauvoo Temple. He was endowed in the Nauvoo Temple 6 January 1846. Mendenhall kept a journal in which he recorded his preparations for leaving Nauvoo.

April 1846 . . .

27th   I sold my house and lot to Julias C. Wright for a wagon, two horse gears and fifty dollars.

28th   Bought my cloth for a tent 60 yards.

29th   Bought a wagon from Br. Burrs.

30th   I helped Mr. Hibbard [that] evening to move [a] fence.

Nauvoo May 1st 1846

May 1st   The Temple was dedicated. [I] took my wagon to the blacksmiths. O.P. Rockwell was taken prisoner.

2nd   I was getting ready to move to the West.

3rd   I was at the dedication of the Temple.

4th   I was planing boards for boxes.

5th   I was planing boards for wagon box.

6th   Wet weather and muddy roads for several days.

7th   I got some iron for wagon went to mill, took wheels to E.L.

8th   I was making boxes to pack goods in.

9th   I was planing boards.

10th   Sunday, was at meeting in the Temple. Mr. J.C. Wright moved in my house.

11th   I brought my wagon home.

12th   I painted my wagon.[63]

# Flats — Main Street

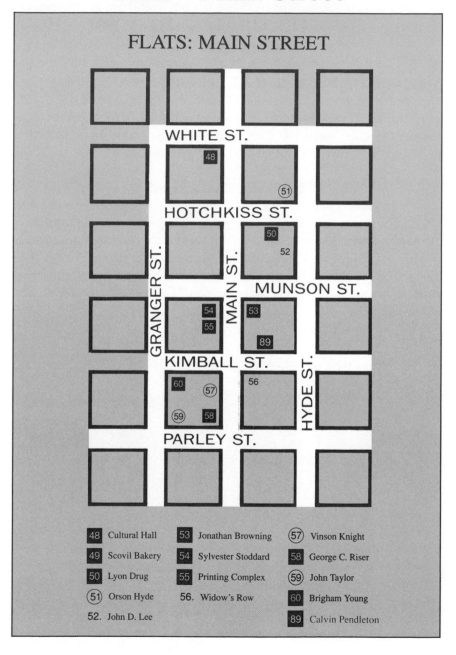

FLATS: MAIN STREET

48 Cultural Hall

49 Scovil Bakery

50 Lyon Drug

51 Orson Hyde

52. John D. Lee

53 Jonathan Browning

54 Sylvester Stoddard

55 Printing Complex

56. Widow's Row

57 Vinson Knight

58 George C. Riser

59 John Taylor

60 Brigham Young

89 Calvin Pendleton

☐

# 48.   THE CULTURAL HALL–MASONIC HALL

The Cultural Hall–Masonic Hall is near the southwest corner of Main and White streets. Extant and reconstructed three-story brick building. This is elegant example of the Federal style. The cornerstone is located at the northeast corner and is inscribed with M.Helm. G.M.A.L.5843 (M. Helm Grandmaster after light 5843, i.e 1843).

### Historical Background

Freemasonry was introduced in Nauvoo on 15 March 1842 when a lodge was organized under the direction of Illinois Grandmaster Abraham Jonas. Many of the leading individuals in Nauvoo, including Joseph Smith, were initiated into Masonry thereafter. The Nauvoo Lodge met occasionally in the upper room of Joseph Smith's General Store previous to the completion of the Masonic Hall in 1844. The

Cultural Hall after third story was removed. Photograph courtesy of LDS Historical Department.

Masonic Temple was dedicated by Hyrum Smith on 5 April 1844 with some five hundred individuals present.

The Cultural/Masonic Hall was used for several purposes besides lodge meetings, including musical and theatrical productions. It was one of the few three-story buildings in Nauvoo at the time. The following article appeared in the Nauvoo newspaper:

> Mr. Editor, taking it as it is, I would ask where are we to go for music, if we do not find it in Nauvoo? I will boldly assert no where. Witness the concert the other evening at the Masonic Hall; got up for the most laudable and praiseworthy purpose. The music in its selection was of the most varied character; and the electrifying feeling that was manifest, proved to a demonstration, that Nauvoo can furnish us with ladies and gentlemen whose instrumental and vocal powers are of no unpolished order. The stringed instruments, the

Cultural Hall recontruction. Photograph courtesy of the authors.

trumpets, flutes, and clarinets, which formed the band, and particularly the flute and violin solos, not only gave a magic charm, but struck the numerous and admiring audience with amaze at the consummate skill they exhibited. We could mention several gentlemen whose talent for music was of the highest order. The songs too, and glees drew forth the most unbounded applause, . . . The ladies will ever be remembered for their sweet, soothing, lively, and harmonious voices, for their graceful appearance, and the choir selection of their pieces. An observer of Men and Things.[64]

There were also plays staged in the Cultural Hall/Masonic Hall, various choirs sang, and Captain Pitt's Brass Band played stirring anthems and Church hymns. A subgroup of the band, the Quadrille Band, enlivened dances, parties, and picnics. Even a city concert hall was built and dedicated in 1843 for musical concerts. Several new hymns were introduced in Nauvoo, including the hymn now known as "A Poor Wayfaring Man of Grief."

□
# 49.  THE SCOVIL BAKERY AND CONFECTIONERY STORE

The Scovil bakery and confectionery store is on the west side of Main between White and Hotchkiss streets. Reconstructed single-story brick building. Notice the ornate spark arrester over the chimney stack.

### Historical Background

Lucius N. Scovil was born 18 March 1806 at Middlebury, New Haven County, Connecticut. He married Lucy Snow 15 June 1824. Scovil was baptized on 2 July 1836. He was endowed in the Nauvoo Temple on 13 December 1845.

His advertisement appeared in the *Nauvoo Neighbor.*

DO YOU KNOW ANY THING ABOUT THE MATTER!
THE subscriber wishes to inform the citizens of Nauvoo and the adjacent towns, that he has established a Bakery and Confectionery,

Scovil Bakery. Photograph courtesy of the authors.

in this city, on Main Street, first door South of the new Masonic Hall, where he intends to manufacture every thing connected with that kind of business—Breads, Crackers, Cakes, Jellys and Candies of all description which he will sell at St. Louis prices wholesale or retail. L.N. SCOVIL

N.B. Marriage cakes made to order on the shortest notice from one to twenty-five dollars each. L.N.S. NAUVOO DEC. 27, 1843.[65]

□

# 50.  THE LYON HOME AND DRUG AND VARIETY STORE

The Lyon home and drug and variety store is on the south side of Hotchkiss between Main and Hyde streets. Extant two-story brick home. Notice the stone lintels over the doors.

## Historical Background
Windsor P. Lyon was born on 8 February 1809 at Orwell, Addison County, Vermont. He married Sylvia P. Sessions in 1838. Lyon was

Lyon Home and Store. Photograph courtesy of LDS Historical Department.

baptized in 1832 in New York. Within a year of his arrival in Nauvoo, Windsor, who was practiced in herbal and botanical medicine, opened a drugstore on the southeast corner on Main and Hotchkiss streets. Lyon constructed a new brick structure east of the old building in 1843. Lyon's new store, as did his wood structure, also served as his family residence. He was endowed in the Nauvoo Temple on 3 February 1846.

The following advertisement indicates that the new store was a general variety store and not just a drug store.

LYON'S STORE SECOND ARRIVAL.

RECEIVED, by the Steamers Osage, Oak, and Rapids, at Lyon's old establishment on the corner of Main and Hotchkiss streets, a splendid stock of New and Genuine GOODS direct from the City of New York, and Philadelphia; and now offered low for cash at wholesale and retail. The stock consists in part as follows. Dry Goods, Groceries, Crockery, Glass, and Hardwares. Books and Stationery, Drugs and Medicines, Paints and Dye stuffs, Boots, Shoes, Military Goods; and a thousand other articles too numerous to mention. Those wishing to make good investments with their money will do well to call at Lyons' cheap cash store, on the corner of Main and Hotchkiss streets.[66]

O

# 51. THE ORSON HYDE HOME

The Orson Hyde home is at the northwest corner of Hotchkiss and Hyde streets. Extant two-story frame home in the Greek Revival style. Notice the unusually heavy corner pilasters.

Orson Hyde home. Photograph courtesy of LDS Historical Department.

## Historical Background

Orson Hyde was born on 8 January 1805 at Oxford, New Haven County, Connecticut. He married Marinda N. Johnson on 4 September 1834. Hyde was baptized on 30 October 1831 at Kirtland, Ohio. He was ordained one of the original members of the Twelve Apostles on 15 February 1835. From Nauvoo he left on a mission to dedicate the Holy Land for the gathering of Israel. He was elected to the Nauvoo Council on 6 February 1843. This home was built for the Hyde family by the citizens of Nauvoo because of Hyde's many years of missionary service for the Church. He was endowed in the upper floor of

Joseph Smith's General Store on 2 December 1843, and in the Nauvoo Temple on 10 December 1845. Hyde offered the prayer at the public dedication of the Nauvoo Temple on 30 April 1846.

In 1844, Hyde's advertisement appeared in the *Nauvoo Neighbor*:

GERMAN BOOKS
ELDER ORSON HYDE would inform the travelling Elders, both German and English, that he has on hand a quantity of pamphlets written in the German language upon the doctrine and principles of the Church of Jesus Christ of Latter-Day Saints, which he will sell very low at his residence in Nauvoo.[67]

*

## 52.   THE JOHN D. LEE HOME SITE

The John D. Lee home was built on the west side of Hyde between Hotchkiss and Munson streets. Nonextant two-story brick home built after the Federal style with Dutch influence on the end walls.

John D. Lee home. Photograph courtesy of Archives and Manuscripts, Harold B. Lee Library, B.Y.U.

**Historical Background**

John D. Lee was born on 6 September 1812 at Kaskaskia, Randolph County, Illinois. He married Agatha A. Woolsey on 23 July 1833 in Illinois. Lee was baptized on 17 June 1837. In Nauvoo he was an agent for the *Nauvoo Neighbor*. He was also the Nauvoo wharf master, a major in the Nauvoo Legion, general clerk and recorder for the Seventies Priesthood Quorum, and served as the clerk for the Temple Committee. He was endowed in the Nauvoo Temple on 11 December 1845.

Lee reluctantly abandoned his home in Nauvoo:

> My large house, costing me $8000 . . . I was offered $800 for. My fanaticism would not allow me to take that for it. I locked it up, selling only one stove out of it, for which I received eighty yards of cloth. The building with its twenty-seven rooms, I turned over to the committee, to be sold to help the poor away. The committee informed afterwards that they sold the house for $12.50.[68]

□
# 53. THE JONATHAN BROWNING HOME AND GUNSHOP

The Jonathan Browning home and gunshop is on the east side of Main between Munson and Kimball streets. Extant and reconstructed two-story brick home and shop on original site. An interesting combination of forms, with Federal influence. Reconstructed two-story frame barn and log cabin built on original site.

**Historical Background**

Jonathan Browning was born on 22 October 1805 at Bushy Fork, Summer County, Tennessee. He married Elizabeth Stalcup on 9 November 1826. Browning was baptized on 10 August 1840 in Adams County, Illinois. Browning sold his gunshop in Quincy, Illinois and moved his family to Nauvoo in 1843. He immediately purchased the half-lot where the home and workshop is located today. Browning was a member of the Nauvoo Library and Literary Institute.

Jonathan Browning home. Photograph courtesy of Nauvoo Historical Society.

□
# 54.   THE SYLVESTER STODDARD HOME AND TINSMITH SHOP

The Sylvester Stoddard tinshop is on the west side of Main between Munson and Kimball streets. Reconstructed two-story brick home typical of the Mormon period.

### Historical Background
· Sylvester Stoddard was born in the early 1800s. He married Almira Knight on 10 November 1844 in Nauvoo, Illinois. Stoddard was apparently baptized sometime between 1833 and 1836.

The following are some extracts from his day account book (September 10, 1840 - January 22, 1842):

1) September 25, 1841 tin on temple $3.24; 2) October 2, 1841 S. Markham 1 six quart bucket 50¢, 2 lbs nails 25¢; Oct. 10, 1841 sold qt. bucket for sugar 50¢; 3) Oct. 26, 1841 Ezra Thompson 8 quart buckets $1.25; 4) Nov. 13, 1841 James Sloan for a bottom on a bucket

Sylvester Stoddard home. Photograph courtesy of LDS Historical Department.

25¢; 5) Dec. 25, 1841 Mr. Weeks 11 lbs of pipe $2.16, stove $23.00; 6) Dec. 27, 1841 James Ivins twelve pound scale $2.50; 7) Dec. 28, 1841 Vinson Knight 1 doz. axes $20.00; 8) Dec. 30, 1841 Hiram Smith iron for fireplace 50; 9) Jan. 1, 1842 T. Turley 5 sheets of tin 32¢; 10) Jan. 1, 1842 S. Markham 1 pair hand irons $1.60; 11) January 4, 1842 J. Smith Jr. 1 fancy stove $21.00, stove pipe 18 1/4 $4.87.[69]

□

# 55.   THE PRINTING COMPLEX

The Printing Complex is on the west side of Main between Munson and Kimball streets. Extant and reconstructed two-story brick home and buildings. This is an interesting complex with a residence in the background. Notice the subordinate relationship of the flanking commercial buildings that form a courtyard.

## Historical Background

James Ivins was born in 1797 in New Jersey. Ivins began building the three red brick structures on this site in April 1842. The first struc-

ture was used as a store, and the second as a residence. The purpose of
the third structure, however, is unknown.

The Church's printing office was housed at several locations before
moving to this site in 1845. The new printing complex contained a
stereotype foundry, typesetting oven, press room, book bindery and
retail bookstore.

When the Mormons left Nauvoo in 1846, A. B. Babbitt, a Church
trustee, used the complex for his residence, for a real estate office to
sell property in Nauvoo for the Church and the Saints who went west,
and for the post office.

John Taylor's journal entry for 13 April 1845 discusses the purchase of the property:

> A man of the name of James Ivins has considerable property, and
> wished to part with it, for the purpose (as he said) of placing his sons
> at some business, not having an opportunity in this place; the con-
> clusion I came to, from his actions, was, that he was disaffected. He
> leaned towards Law when he was cut off; when Rigdon went the
> same way he had such another leaning. In consequence of these the
> people lost all confidence in him, and he knowing it, was desirous of

Printing Complex. Photograph courtesy of LDS Historical Department.

leaving. He had a first rate large brick house, brick store, and large pine board barn, on a half acre of land on Main street, corner of Kimball, which he had offered to me for three thousand two hundred dollars although the buildings had cost twice that sum. I asked the brethren what their counsel was upon the subject; they said go ahead and get it. I took measures forthwith to procure it, not that I wanted to build myself up; but my idea in getting it was to keep it out of the hands of our enemies, as it was offered so cheap; and I thought the store would suit us for a Printing office. My feelings after I had traded for this were the same as ever, I felt like sacrificing all things when called upon, my heart is not set upon property, but the things of God: I care not so much about the good things of this life, as I do about the fellowship of my brethren, and to fulfilling the word the Lord has called me to do; and the favor of the Lord, and securing to myself, my family, and friends an inheritance in the Kingdom of God. Moved into the house May 10, 1845.[70]

## *
## 56. THE WIDOW'S ROW (BRICK ROW) SITE

The Widow's Row (Brick Row) was built near the southwest corner of Main and Kimball streets. Nonextant single-story brick building.

### Historical Background

A group of buildings known as "Widow's Row" or "Brick Row" backed-up on an alley. Some of the tenants included: Lorenzo Booth, Elizabeth Kendall, Sophia Leyland, George Mardist, Washington Myres, and John S. Roph.

Elizabeth Kendall, a widow of John Kendall and mother of three children, arrived in Nauvoo in February 1843 from England.

They landed at the upper landing in Nauvoo. . . . she hustled about finding a place to leave her children and securing information from those who were there to give it. Indeed her feet were weary for a brisk walk, and eagerly she started for the city more than a mile away. . . . she found on the corner of Main and Kimball streets a long, one-story brick building, built with its front to the west where a door opened to Main street; parallel with Kimball street it ran back towards the east. Ten comfortable rooms with doors opening into the garden plot, each room with such a door, two windows and a fireplace. This was a tenement owned by a widow, whose tenants were preferably widows . . . [she] secured the third room from the east end . . . returned to the landing for her children and her early store of goods; putting them in the room she now called home, she went buoyantly about the town seeking work.[71]

Widow's Row. Photograph courtesy of LDS Historical Department.

Looking at the intersection of Main and Kimball streets. Photograph courtesy of Nauvoo Historical Society.

O

# 57. THE VINSON KNIGHT HOME

The Vinson Knight home is on the west side of Main between Kimball and Parley streets. Extant two-story brick home. Notice the unusual lack of symmetry with one window missing above the entry.

### Historical Background

Vinson Knight was born on 14 March 1804 at Norwich, Hampshire County, Massachusetts. He married Martha McBride on 14 March 1826. Knight was baptized in 1834. Vinson Knight was appointed Bishop over the lower Nauvoo Ward on 5 October 1839. He was a member of the city council and the Nauvoo Agricultural and Manufacturing Association. On 19 January 1841, he was designated by revelation to be Presiding Bishop of the Church (LDS D&C 124:141/RLDS D&C 107:45). He died in Nauvoo on 31 July 1842, just five months after he wrote the letter below. He was endowed

Vinson Knight home. Photograph courtesy of LDS Historical Department.

before July 1843. In February 1842, Vinson wrote to his family back East:

> City of Nauvoo February 14, 1842
> We have not had any sleighing and the weather most of the time has been mild and all things seem to move in good order and good feelings. I think we have no reason to complain, but on the other hand to rejoice and praise God . . . My family are in good health at this time. The children are all glad to hear from Grandmother and all their relations. Martha and all the children send their love to you. Rodophus E. [a son] grows finely. The children all love him and sometimes cry to hold him. I wish you could see him. You would say that he was a fine boy.[72]

☐

# 58.   THE RISER BOOT AND SHOEMAKER SHOP

The Riser Boot and Shoemaker Shop is near the northwest corner of Main and Parley streets. Reconstructed two-story brick home.

### Historical Background
George C. Riser was born on 16 July 1818 at Chornwesthaem, Wurttemburg, Germany. He married Christinana Knell on 10 January 1841. Riser was baptized on 12 December 1842 in the Mississippi River at Nauvoo. He was endowed in the Nauvoo Temple on 5 January 1846.

George Riser relates in his reminiscence several personal experiences after his arrival in Nauvoo on 4 October 1842.

> Dec. 11th [1842] my little child; John, was sick nigh to death. I was led to send for Joseph the Prophet to lay hands on him. Elder Orson Hyde accompanied him. Joseph advised us to keep the child in a room that was not so hot and predicted that he would recover; which he instantly did as soon as they took their hands from him. . . .
> Joseph and Elder Orson Hyde, who had then lately returned from Jerusalem, called into the adjoining room . . . the door being left open, I could hear the conversation. Elder Hyde spoke of some things relative to his mission — said that while in company with some of the leading Jews they became somewhat merry and exhilarated,

George Riser home. Photograph courtesy of the authors.

drinking wine and smoking. They said to him, "Mr. Hyde, I'd be blamed if we won't do anything you may tell us." Brother Joseph told Brother Hyde that was the time he ought to have gathered the Jews.

The jocose conversation so contrary to my notions of the character of a prophet and saints, caused me to think soberly, but upon reflection I could not think of anything they had said but what was innocent and I felt that a prophet had a right to enjoy himself innocently as well as any other person. I then concluded to be baptized. My wife also came to the same conclusions, and we were baptized the following day December 12, 1842 by Elder Albert Brown in the Mississippi River. The weather was extremely cold. The river was so frozen that a hole had to be cut in the ice to baptize us in. . . . We were confirmed the same day at our residence by the same Elder.

During the winter, I worked at my trade and improved every opportunity to hear preaching that I might the better become acquainted with the doctrine and principles of the Church. The winter was extremely cold. The following spring my little boy, John, was again taken very ill. I had him administered to by a number of

Elders, among whom were two of the Apostles, . . . Brother Joseph called . . . I again asked him to administer to the child, but for some cause he was not led to make the same promise of life as before. He died on the 6th of May at the age of fourteen months and was buried the next day.[73]

O

## 59.  THE JOHN TAYLOR MARKER

The John Taylor marker is located on the north side of Parley between Main and Granger streets.

### Historical Background

John Taylor was born on 1 November 1808 at Milnthorpe, Westmoreland, England. He married Leonora Cannon on 28 January 1833 in Toronto, Canada. Taylor was baptized on 9 May 1836 in Toronto, Canada. In Nauvoo he served on the Nauvoo City Council, in the Nauvoo Legion and as a regent of Nauvoo University. He was also the editor-in-chief of the *Times and Seasons* from 1842–1846 and editor and proprietor of the *Nauvoo Neighbor* from May 1843–October 1845. Taylor lived at this site before moving to the printing complex in 1845. He was endowed in the upper floor of Joseph Smith's General Store on 28 September 1843 and in the Nauvoo Temple on 10 December 1845. Taylor was shot four times during the Carthage attack. He later became the third president of the LDS Church, ordained in Salt Lake City, Utah on 10 October 1880.

Wilford Woodruff recorded a visit with Taylor shortly after the Carthage shooting:

> August 7th, 1844. I went forth this morning through the city of Nauvoo. Saw many friends and met with the quorum of the twelve at Elder Taylor's. We were truly glad to see each other. Brother Taylor was getting well of his wounds that he received in jail in company with Joseph and Hyrum Smith when they were murdered. We were glad to see Dr. Richards who escaped unhurt. We were received with gladness by the Saints throughout the city. They felt like sheep without a shepherd, as being without a father, as their head had been taken away. We spent the fore part of the day at Brother Taylors.[74]

☐
# 60. THE BRIGHAM YOUNG HOME

The Brigham Young home is near the southeast corner of Granger and Kimball streets. Extant two-story brick home erected in 1843 with wings added in 1844; its crow-step roof reflects the influence of old Dutch homes in New York.

Brigham Young home. Photograph courtesy of LDS Historical Department.

## Historical Background

Brigham Young was born on 1 June 1801 at Whittingham, Windham County, Vermont. He married Miriam Works on 8 October 1824 at Port Bryon, New York. Young was baptized on 14 April 1832 at Mendon, New York. While he was in missionary service to the British Isles, his wife secured the present building site. "When I returned from England," Brigham wrote, "my family was living in a small unfurnished log-cabin, situated on a low, wet lot, so swampy that when the first attempt was made to plow it the oxen mired." On 31 May 1843 he wrote in his journal, "I moved out of my log cabin into my new brick house, which was 22 feet by 16, two stories high, and a good cellar under it, and felt thankful to God for the privilege of having a comfortable though small habitation."[75] He was endowed in the upper floor of the Joseph Smith General Store on 4 May 1842, and in the Nauvoo Temple on 10 December 1845. Young was ordained second president of the LDS Church on 27 December 1847 in Council Bluffs, Iowa.

Several months after the death of Joseph and Hyrum Smith, the question of whether or not the Saints should remain in Nauvoo and finish the temple or seek some other place to gather was facing Church leaders. In January 1845 Brigham Young recorded the following in his journal:

> Friday, January 24. Brothers Heber C. Kimball and Newell K. Whitney were at my house. We washed, anointed, and prayed. Had a good time. I inquired of the Lord whether we should stay here and finish the Temple. The answer was we should.[76]

□

# 89. CALVIN PENDLETON HOME AND SCHOOLHOUSE

The Calvin Pendleton home and schoolhouse is on the north side of Kimball between Main and Hyde streets. Reconstructed single-story log cabin.

## Historical Background

Calvin Pendleton was born on 25 August 1811 at Hope, Knox County, Maine. He married Salley Ann Seavey on 29 October 1843 at Nauvoo, Illinois. Pendleton was baptized in 1838. He was endowed in the Nauvoo Temple on 17 December 1845.

# Flats — Southwest

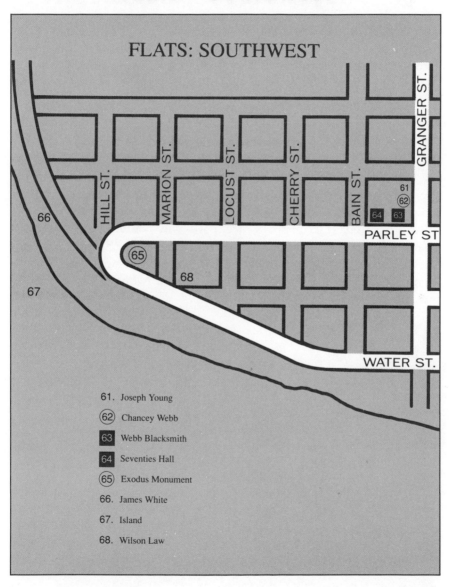

FLATS: SOUTHWEST

61. Joseph Young
62. Chancey Webb
63. Webb Blacksmith
64. Seventies Hall
65. Exodus Monument
66. James White
67. Island
68. Wilson Law

*

# 61.  THE JOSEPH YOUNG HOME SITE

The Joseph Young home was built on the west side of Granger between Kimball and Parley streets. Nonextant one and a half-story home with a roof monitor. Although the cornice is Greek Revival in character, the use of a hipped roof and extended chimney stacks is more typical of the Colonial Georgian period, perhaps derived from an older carpenter's manual.

### Historical Background

Joseph W. Young was born on 7 April 1797 in Hopkinton, Middlesex County, Massachusetts. He married Jane A. Bicknell on 18 February 1834 at Kirtland, Ohio. Young was baptized on 6 April 1832 at Columbia, Pennsylvania. The Young family moved to Nauvoo in the Spring of 1840. His primary occupation in Nauvoo was that of a painter/glazer. Young served as the president of the Seventies priesthood quorum. He was endowed in the upper floor of Joseph Smith's General Store on 3 February 1844 and in the Nauvoo Temple on 12 December 1845.

Joseph Young home. Photograph courtesy of Harold Allen.

○
## 62. THE CHAUNCEY WEBB HOME

The Chauncey Webb home is on the west side of Granger between Kimball and Parley streets. Extant single-story brick home.

### Historical Background

Chauncey Webb was born on 24 October 1812 at Hanover, Chautauqua County, New York. He married Eliza J. Churchill on 16 September 1834 at Kirtland, Ohio. Webb was baptized on 24 November 1834. He was a member of the Nauvoo Seventies priesthood quorum and the Nauvoo Library and Literary Institute. He was endowed in the Nauvoo Temple on 16 December 1845.

Chauncey Webb home (nearest); Joseph Young home (middle). Photograph courtesy of Archives and Manuscripts, Harold B. Lee Library, B.Y.U.

□
## 63. THE WEBB BLACKSMITH SHOP

The Webb blacksmith shop is on the north side of Parley between Granger and Bain streets. Reconstructed single-story stone building on original site.

Webb's Blacksmith Shop. Photograph courtesy of the authors.

### Historical Background

Edwin D. Webb was born in 1813 at Hanover, Chautaugne County, New York. He married Eliza Ann McGuinthy on 13 December 1835 in Kirtland, Ohio. Webb was probably baptized in 1834 along with most of his brothers. The Webb Blacksmith Shop was one of the hubs of the city in 1845–1846. The Webb brothers built numerous wagons to assist the Saints in leaving for the west. Chauncey and Edwin Webb were still working in Nauvoo in September 1846.

This advertisement appeared in the *Nauvoo Neighbor*:

LET US DO AS WE OUGHT.

THE subscriber would respectfully inform the citizens of Nauvoo and vicinity that he has recently commenced the Blacksmithing business in his stone-shop, where he will be happy to accommodate all that favor him with a call; and feeling as he does that he can and will give general satisfaction to all reasonable men, as he has a journeyman of long experience. The subscriber will furnish stock to any amount if wished, on the most reasonable terms; at very little above St. Louis prices.

N.B. All orders from the country promptly attended to. Country produce of all kinds taken in payment for work, and small quantity of cash will not be refused. EDWIN D. WEBB.[77]

☐
# 64. THE SEVENTIES HALL

The Seventies Hall is at the northeast corner of Parley and Bain streets. Reconstructed two-story brick building on original site. Notice the glazed fanlight over the door. An inscription stone on the front facade reads "Priesthood."

## Historical Background

The Seventies were a priesthood group within the Church with responsibility for missionary work. The bottom floor of the hall was used for classes (including fencing), lectures, and worship. The second floor housed the town library. Edward Hunter donated the lot. The construction was halted temporarily because a tornado destroyed one side in 1844. The new building was ready for use in July 1844. The first of several dedicatory services was held on 26 December 1844. John Taylor described that particular dedication service:

> Thursday, December 26th, 1844. I attended the dedication of the Seventies Hall. The services commenced under the direction of President Joseph Young, who organized the meeting in the following

Seventies Hall after second story was removed. Photograph courtesy of LDS Historical Department.

order. The stand was occupied by the seven presiding presidents of the Seventies; and the Twelve or as many of them as were present. The senior president of Quorum was seated on the right, the choir of singers on the left, and the brass band in front. The second and third quorums in order, with their families, might in turn participate in the privilege of the dedication, according to their respective quorums, there being fifteen quorums, whose claims were equal, two of which convened in the Hall each day, beginning with the second and third. The excellent melody of the choir and Band, mingled with the devout aspirations of a congregation of *all Saints*, gave the commencement of their services an air of interest, felicity, and glory, at once feeling, touching, pathetic, grand, and sublime.[78]

Seventies Hall after reconstruction. Photograph courtesy of the authors.

O

# 65.  THE EXODUS TO GREATNESS
# MONUMENT AND FERRY CROSSING

The Exodus to Greatness Monument is on the south side of Parley
near the end of the gravel road. The Ferry Crossing is located at the
west end of Parley at the Mississippi River.

### Historical Background

Charles Shumway arrived at the Nauvoo Ferry Crossing very early
on 4 February 1846. As he waited in nearly zero degree weather at the
foot of Parley Street with his ox-drawn wagon, Shumway must have
considered the beautiful city he was leaving behind and the uncertain
destination of his journey ahead. Soon he began his famous trip across
the Mississippi River, the first of many who would follow in the next
days, weeks, and months. The crossing occurred with the help of flat-
bottomed ferry boats, designed to carry one wagon and propelled by
paddle wheels. Later, during a brief period, the river froze which
allowed the wagons to cross the river on the ice.

The ferrymen worked throughout the first days tirelessly moving
their cargo to Montrose. An accident endangered several individuals
as they attempted to ford the river a few days later. Brigham Young
related the following in his journal:

> A number of brethren were crossing the river in a flatboat, when in
> their rear a man and two boys were in a skiff in a sinking condition,
> on account of being overloaded and the unskillfulness of the helms-
> man. They hailed to the flatboat, which was soon turned, and ren-
> dered them assistance. As soon as they had got the three on board
> the flatboat, a filthy wicked man squirted some tobacco juice into
> the eyes of one of the oxen . . . which immediately plunged into the
> river, dragging another with him, and as he was going overboard he
> tore off one of the sideboards which caused the water to flow into the
> flatboat, and as they approached the shore the boat sank to the bot-
> tom, before all the men could leap off. Several of the brethren were
> picked up in an exhausted condition. Two oxen were drowned and a
> few things floated away and were lost.[79]

*

# 66.  THE JAMES WHITE HOME SITE

The James White home was built on the north side of Parley beyond the end of the street. The site of the White home is presently underwater. Nonextant two-story stone home.

### Historical Background

James White was born on 10 June 1782 in Vermont. He married Lurancy Barber. The "trading oak" of legend was located near his home. The white stone building was built in 1827. He died in Commerce (Nauvoo) on 15 June 1836.

Traditionally, the "trading oak" in Nauvoo was identified as the place where in 1823 Captain James White traded 200 bags of corn to the Indians for the area known as Quashquema.[80] White and his family are considered the first permanent white settlers of the area. Other settlers established homes and farms soon after.

Hancock County was organized in 1829, and a post office, called Venus, was established near the White home. This post office served

James White home. Photograph courtesy of LDS Historical Department.

two dozen families in the area by 1830. The village of Venus served as the first county seat of Hancock County, but the administration was subsequently moved to Carthage, which was the geographical center of the county. Venus continued to grow during this period.

In 1839 Isaac Galland was living in Commerce in the home of James White, which he had purchased sometime during the winter. In the fall Galland met Israel Barlow, a Mormon who had recently arrived in Iowa from Missouri. This first contact with the Mormons would lead Galland to sell huge tracts of land to the destitute Saints at very reasonable terms.

This home served as Sidney Rigdon's residence upon his arrival at Commerce (Nauvoo) in 1839. Later, the home was known as the Nauvoo Ferry Hotel, managed by Charles Ivins and S. Bennett. This advertisement appeared in the *Times and Seasons*:

### NAUVOO FERRY HOTEL

S. Bennett, having the occupancy of the Stone House, recently in the possession of Sidney Rigdon, will appropriate it as a HOUSE OF ENTERTAINMENT. Travelers and resident boarders, shall be well treated and reasonably charged. Commodious stabling on the premises. August 2, 1841.[81]

James White Home partially submerged by the Mississippi River after the construction of the Keokok Dam in 1913. Photograph courtesy of LDS Historical Dept.

The Stone House was near the site of one of the city's steamboat landings. Residents of Nauvoo often left the city for visits to friends, family members, or on Church, civic, or personal business. Their return to Nauvoo was always something highly anticipated. Shortly after her husband's death, Louisa Follett left Nauvoo to visit family back East. She recorded her feelings about her return to Nauvoo on 5 September 1845. She then described her landing at the Stone House:

> Oh how I long to gaze one more [time] on the beloved City of the Saints and meet the warm embrace of my children and friends. I have left Babylon for the last time, and thanks be to God for his preserving care during my long and protracted journey.
> Sunday 7 September 1845
> At length we got safe over [the rapids] which brought [us] in sight of the beloved City. . . . At ten o'clock we safely landed at the Stone House where we meet with the most cordial welcome from our friends and relatives in Nauvoo. . . . Although my health is much impaired yet when I take a retrospective view of the past, I feel that I have abundant reason to bless God that amidst the danger to which I have been exposed that I have been mercifully preserved and brought to join my afflicted family and brethren in Nauvoo.[82]

*

# 67.  THE ISLAND

The Island has been under water since the Mississippi river rose more than twenty-two feet after the construction of the Keokuk Dam in 1913.

### Historical Background

At least two timbered-covered islands stood in the river between Montrose and Nauvoo. By 1909 these islands were called Kimball and Galland Islands, named after Heber C. Kimball and Isaac Galland.[83] The islands were used for the wood resources they contained and by Joseph Smith as a retreat during periods of persecution.

The prophet's journal records a secret meeting in August 1842 on one of these islands:

> How good and glorious, it has seemed unto me, to find pure and holy friends. . . . How glorious were my feelings when I met that faithful and friendly band, on the night of the eleventh on thursday,

Island off Nauvoo. Photograph courtesy of Nauvoo Historical Society.

on the Island, at the mouth of the slough, between Zarahemla and Nauvoo. With what unspeakable delight, and what transports of joy swelled my bosom, when I took by the hand on that night, my beloved Emma, she that was my wife, even the wife of my youth, and the choice of my heart. . . . Many were the thoughts that swelled my aching heart, while [the men who took Joseph to the island and returned him] were toiling faithfully with their oars. They complained not of hardship and fatigue to secure my safety.[84]

*

# 68. THE WILSON LAW HOME SITE

The Wilson Law home was built on the north side of Water Street. Nonextant two-story brick home. It was a pure expression of the Federal style. Notice in the photo the entrance motif, and other typical Federal features.

## Historical Background

Wilson Law was born in 1807. He married Elizabeth Sikes on 25 December 1842. Law was baptized in Nauvoo. He was a member of the Nauvoo Legion and a city alderman. Law assisted in organizing a dissident church on 28 April 1844 in Nauvoo. He was involved in the writing and publication of the *Nauvoo Expositor* in June 1844.

James Blakeslee wrote a brief account of the organization meeting of this dissident church:

On the 28th of April 1844, several of the Saints met in conference at the house of Messrs. Wilson and William Law in Nauvoo and organized a branch of the Church of Jesus Christ of Latter Day Saints by duly appointing President William Law presiding Elder and Austin Cowles and James Blakeslee his counselors. Charles Ivins [appointed] Bishop and J.Y. Green and Jacob Scott his counselors who together with President Law and his Counselors were all ordained and set apart to their respective offices by a unanimous vote. Brother J.M. Cole was appointed secretary; and we commenced preaching in Nauvoo, and in other places as the Lord gave ability with some success, and in order to send the truth more speedily to the world than we could otherwise.[85]

William Law, appointed president of this church named the "Church of Jesus Christ," recorded in his diary an account of an early meeting that took place at his brother's home.

The evening of this day I spent at my brother Wilson Law's, a small party of friends were assembled there, and after partaking of an excellent supper, we conversed upon various subjects, amongst the rest the Doctrine (so called) of plurality [of wives] . . . they were strongly [disapproved], refreshment we returned home.[86]

Traditionally identified as the Wilson Law home. Photograph courtesy of LDS Historical Department.

# Flats—Water Street

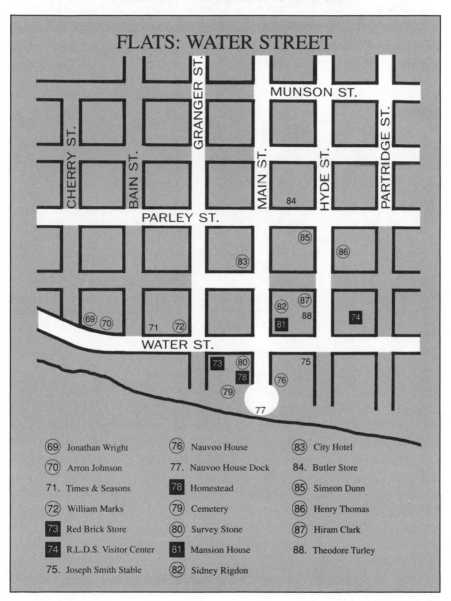

FLATS: WATER STREET

| | | |
|---|---|---|
| ⑥⑨ Jonathan Wright | ⑦⑥ Nauvoo House | ⑧③ City Hotel |
| ⑦⓪ Arron Johnson | 77. Nauvoo House Dock | 84. Butler Store |
| 71. Times & Seasons | ▐78▌ Homestead | ⑧⑤ Simeon Dunn |
| ⑦② William Marks | ⑦⑨ Cemetery | ⑧⑥ Henry Thomas |
| ▐73▌ Red Brick Store | ⑧⓪ Survey Stone | ⑧⑦ Hiram Clark |
| ▐74▌ R.L.D.S. Visitor Center | ▐81▌ Mansion House | 88. Theodore Turley |
| 75. Joseph Smith Stable | ⑧② Sidney Rigdon | |

O
# 69. THE JONATHAN WRIGHT HOME

The Jonathan Wright home is on the north side of Water near Bain Street. Extant two-story brick home.

Water Street–Jonathan Wright home (on the left). Photograph courtesy of LDS Historical Department.

### Historical Background

Jonathan C. Wright was born 29 November 1805 at Rome, Oneida County, New York. He married Rebecca Wheeler on 1 March 1838 at Waynesville, Illinois. Wright was baptized 29 May 1843 in the Mississippi River at Nauvoo, Illinois. He was a county commissioner and prosperous businessman at Exeter, Scott County, Illinois before moving to Nauvoo. In Nauvoo he acted as marshall and was a member of the city council. He was endowed in the Nauvoo Temple on 31 December 1845.

O
# 70. THE AARON JOHNSON HOME

The Aaron Johnson home is near the northwest corner of Water and

Aaron Johnson home (nearest). Photograph courtesy of LDS Historical Department.

Bain streets. Extant two-story brick home. The entrance motif is not a typical style.

### Historical Background

Aaron Johnson was born 22 June 1806 at Haddam, Middlesex County, Connecticut. He married Polly Z. Kelsey 13 September 1827 at New Haven, Connecticut. Johnson was baptized on 15 April 1836. He moved to Nauvoo sometime in 1839. He was appointed to the building committee for the Nauvoo Masonic Hall and Justice of the Peace in Nauvoo. He was called to be a member of the Nauvoo High Council on 19 January 1841 and was also a member of the Nauvoo Library and Literary Institute. He was endowed in the Nauvoo Temple on 12 December 1845.

Aaron owned a farm across the Mississippi River in Iowa. He had a small boat which he used regularly to cross the river. This boat was tied up to a small dock in front of his home. At about 2 A.M. in the morning on 23 June 1844 Joseph, Hyrum, Orrin Porter Rockwell, and Willard Richards walked along Water Street to Aaron Johnson's home. When they found Aaron's boat they got in and rowed across the river. The prophet was in hiding again just prior to his murder a few days later in Carthage. Joseph's *History* records what happened next as they crossed the river:

O.P. Rockwell rowed the skiff, which was very leaky, so that it kept Joseph, Hyrum, and the Doctor busy baling out the water with their boots and shoes to prevent it from sinking. At daybreak they arrived on the Iowa side.[87]

*

# 71.   THE TIMES AND SEASONS BUILDING FOUNDATION

The Times and Seasons building foundation is at the northeast corner of Water and Bain streets. Nonextant one and half-story frame building.

### Historical Background

*The Times and Seasons* was published in at least three locations at Nauvoo. The paper was published from 1839 to 1841 at this site, first in a warehouse and later in a wooden structure built here. From 1841–1845 it was published across the street at the northwest corner

Traditionally identified as the first Times and Seasons Building. Photograph courtesy of RLDS Graphic Design Commission.

of Water and Bain streets. John Taylor moved the publishing establishment to the west side of Main between Kimball and Parley streets in 1845.[88]

Ebenezer Robinson, who worked with the paper during part of this time, wrote:

> The only room that could be obtained for the printing office [in 1839], was a basement room in a building formerly used as a warehouse. . . . it had no floor, and the ground was kept damp by the water constantly trickling down the bank side. Here we set type for the first number of the paper . . . a small, cheap frame building [was] put up, one and a half stories high, the lower room to be used for the printing office, and . . . the upper room [for my family].[89]

At this printing establishment and at the printing complex on Main Street, the Saints in Nauvoo not only published several newspapers, but also other Church publications. In 1840 Joseph Smith published the third edition of the *Book of Mormon* in Nauvoo. It was "carefully revised by the translator." A fourth edition was printed by Joseph Smith in 1842. It was during this period that Joseph Smith stated: "I told the brethren that the Book of Mormon was the most correct of any book on earth, and the keystone of our religion, and a man would get nearer to God by abiding by its precepts, than by any other book."[90]

A second edition of the *Doctrine and Covenants* was published in 1844; a third edition was printed in 1845; and a fourth edition in 1846.

O

## 72. THE WILLIAM MARKS HOME

The William Marks home is on the north side of Water between Bain and Granger streets. Extant two-story brick home. Notice the chimney stacks are set back from the end wall, typical of the New England style.

### Historical Background

William Marks was born on 15 November 1792 at Rutland, Rutland County, Vermont. He married Rosannah Robinson on 2 May 1813. Marks was baptized shortly before April 1835 at Portage, New York. He was appointed as the president of the Nauvoo Stake on 5 October

William Marks home. Photograph courtesy of RLDS Graphic Design Commission.

1839 and was elected as a Nauvoo city alderman. He was endowed in the upper room of Joseph Smith's General Store on 4 May 1842. Marks was a member of the RLDS Church First Presidency along with Joseph Smith III at Plano, Illinois.

Joseph Smith visited the Marks home on 13 January 1843: "Went to Brother William Marks to see Sophia who was sick. Heard her relate the vision or dream of a visit from her two brothers who were dead—touching the associations and relations of another world."[91]

□

# 73.  THE JOSEPH SMITH GENERAL STORE (RED BRICK STORE)

The Joseph Smith General Store (Red Brick Store) is on the south side of Water near Granger Street. Reconstructed two-story brick building on original site. It is typical of commercial buildings built in the Greek Revival style with large glazed doors across the front that can be opened in summer.

Joseph Smith General Store (Red Brick Store). Photograph courtesy of RLDS Graphic Design Commission.

## Historical Background

The store opened for business on 5 January 1842, but Joseph Smith was unable to have an active role in its management after 1842. The first story of the store was primarily dedicated to business. The second story was used by a number of associations and organizations, including the Nauvoo Temple Committee, the Nauvoo House Committee, the Nauvoo City Council, the Nauvoo Legion for court martials, the Nauvoo Masonic Lodge, the Nauvoo Female Relief Society, and various priesthood quorums. The room was also used for blessing meetings, and for school classes. The store was also the Church and city administrative office building in Nauvoo.

Joseph Smith's journal for 1842 includes the following entries:

[17 March 1842] [I assisted in commencing the organization of the Female] Relief Society of Nauvoo in the Lodge Room. Sister Emma Smith, President, and Sisters Elizabeth Ann Whitney and Sarah M. Cleveland Counselors. I gave much instruction, read in the New Testament [2 John 1], and Book of Doctrine and Covenants [LDS 25 and RLDS 24 ] concerning the Elect Lady, and showed that the elect meant to be elected to a certain work etc. and that the revelation was then fulfilled by Sister Emma's election to the Presidency of the Society, she having previously been ordained to expound Scriptures. [Emma was blessed, and her counselors were ordained by Elder John Taylor.][92]

[28 April 1842] [At two o'clock P.M. I met] the members of the Female Relief Society and after presiding at the admission of many new members gave a lecture on the Priesthood showing how the sisters would come in possession of the privileges, blessings, and gifts

Joseph Smith General Store (Red Brick Store) c. 1885. Photograph courtesy of Kenneth E. Stobaugh.

of the Priesthood, and that the signs should follow them, such as healing the sick, casting out devils etc. and that they might attain unto these blessings by a virtuous life and conversation and diligence in keeping all the commandments.[93]

The Nauvoo Relief Society minutes add this information:

He [Joseph] did not know as he should have many opportunities of teaching them—that they were going to be left to themselves—they would not long have him to instruct them—that the church would not have his instruction long, and the world would not be troubled with him a great while, and would not have his teachings. He spoke of delivering the keys to this society and to the Church—that according to his prayers God had appointed him elsewhere. . . . that the keys of the kingdom are about to be given to them, that they may be able to detect everything false—as well as the Elders. . . . I now turn the key to you in the name of God and this Society shall rejoice, and knowledge and intelligence shall flow down from this time—this is the beginning of better days to this Society.[94]

These keys of the kingdom would be given to the body of the Church in the planned temple that would be the focus of the prophet's work until his death in 1844. The temple would serve a dual function, not only as a general meeting house like the Kirtland Temple before, but as a place where God would reveal "the fulness of the priesthood. . . . [the Lord's] ordinances . . . things which have been kept hid from before the foundation of the world, things that pertain to the dispensation of the fulness of times."[95]

Anticipated religious ordinances to be performed in the temple included baptisms for the dead; washings and anointings; endowments; prayer circles; sealings, including marriages for time and eternity; and priesthood adoptions.[96] Before the temple was completed, the prophet introduced these ordinances to a small group of followers in the second story of this store, or on the second floor of the Homestead, or from his new home, the Nauvoo Mansion. Beginning in May 1842, and during the next twenty-two months, several other men and women received their endowments and sealings under the direction of Joseph and Emma Smith.

☐

# 74.  THE JOSEPH SMITH HISTORIC CENTER VISITOR CENTER (RLDS CHURCH)

The Joseph Smith Historic Center Visitor Center (RLDS Church) is on the north side of Water between Hyde and Partridge streets.

### Historical Background

The RLDS Church visitor center was built in 1979–1980 and dedicated on 3 May 1980. The complex includes a bookstore, a rotating display of Nauvoo period antiques, and an auditorium where an introductory film is shown. It is the starting point for the walking tour of the Joseph Smith historic district properties (Joseph Smith Homestead and Nauvoo Mansion).

The RLDS Church is the largest of several groups that did not accept the leadership of Brigham Young and the Twelve Apostles. Some of these groups eventually settled in western Iowa, southern Wisconsin, and Illinois. Jason Briggs and Zenos Gurley, Jr., were leaders of an alternative group that was originally called the "New Organization." Founded in 1853 by Jason Briggs, who was the first president of the Quorum of Apostles, the Reorganization eventually attracted several of Joseph Smith's family to its ranks in the 1860s.[97]

Emma Smith, Joseph's widow, fled Nauvoo on 12 September 1846 to Fulton City, Illinois, 120 miles to the north. Her small family included Joseph III, Alexander, Julia, and David Hyrum, born on 19 November 1844. Emma eventually returned to her home in Nauvoo to raise her children. This period of time was very stressful for Emma as she attempted to gain some stability and financial security. In 1847 she married Lewis Bidamon. Her oldest son, Joseph Smith III, became the first president of the Reorganized Church of Jesus Christ of Latter Day Saints at their general conference in 1860. Two other sons, Alexander and David Hyrum, also played significant roles in this organization.

The Joseph Smith Homestead and the Mansion House have belonged to the Smith family since the death of Joseph in 1844. The Smith properties were deeded over to the RLDS Church in 1915. Soon thereafter, the RLDS Church sent caretakers, John W. Layton and his wife Ida, to move into the Mansion House in 1918. That same year the RLDS Church began to restore the Smith properties, which had deteriorated badly during the intervening years, and opened them for visits. F. M. Smith, RLDS Church president, ordered an attempt to find the bodies of Joseph and Hyrum Smith. The graves were found on 22 January 1928. Now marked, these graves have become an important part of the RLDS Church's restoration and preservation project, which includes approximately fifty acres of old Nauvoo, and several residences now known as the Joseph Smith Historic Center.[98]

*

# 75.  THE JOSEPH SMITH BRICK STABLE FOUNDATION

The Joseph Smith brick stable foundation is at the southwest corner of Water and Hyde streets. Nonextant two-story brick building.

The Joseph Smith Brick Stable (on the right). Photograph of painting courtesy of RLDS Graphic Design Commission.

### Historical Background

Along with the Nauvoo Mansion house, Joseph Smith constructed a large brick stable capable of boarding up to seventy-five horses and requisite forage.[99] In 1841, the Twelve Apostles reported that Joseph Smith was himself despoiled of his personal property in Missouri. They said his property consisted of only "his old Charley (a horse) given him in Kirtland, two pet deer, two old turkeys and four young ones, the old cow given him by a brother in Missouri, his old Major, (a dog) . . . and a little household furniture."[100] His horse Charley, and another horse purchased in Nauvoo, Joe Duncan, were two of his favorite horses and were well known to both those in and outside of the Church.

George Q. Cannon, a resident of Nauvoo, recalled a story about Joseph Smith and his horse, Charley:

> The Prophet had a great fondness for animals. His horse Charley was widely known among the people, and with the boys of Nauvoo he was a great favorite. . . . [I am reminded of] an occurrence which created considerable amusement at the time. A boy named Wesley Cowle was flying a kite in one of the streets of Nauvoo. One or two strangers came up to him and asked him where the Prophet could be found. At that time officers were said to be coming from Carthage for the purpose of serving papers upon Joseph and arresting him. "Wes" Cowle did not know but the strangers were officers. He said the Prophet was not in the city. He and Hyrum had gone to heaven on "old Charley" and he was flying his kite to send them their dinner.[101]

○

# 76.   THE NAUVOO HOUSE

The Nauvoo House is near the south end of Main Street. Initial portion of a much larger structure built with stone and brick in a nontraditional style, but reflects the Federal architectural influence.

### Historical Background

The revelation contained in LDS D&C 124 and RLDS D&C 107 commanded the Saints to build the Nauvoo House to provide housing for visitors to the city. On 23 February 1841 a committee was orga-

Nauvoo House, with original north wing. Photograph courtesy of Buddy Youngreen.

nized to oversee the hotel's construction. Since the building was estimated to cost approximately $150,000 the Saints decided to issue stock to finance the construction. Joseph Smith donated the land for the hotel, and in return he and his descendants were to receive rooms in the structure for their perpetual use.

The Nauvoo House was designed to be shaped in the form of an "L", with two 120-foot wings, a depth of 40 feet and three stories. The bodies of Joseph and Hyrum Smith were secretly buried here before their internment at the Smith family cemetery across the street. Work progressed sporadically and slowly because of a lack of funds, although there was a last effort to complete the building on 18 August 1845. Shortly thereafter the work on the Nauvoo House was discontinued in an effort to finish the temple. Construction of the Nauvoo House walls reached the second-floor in 1846, but was never finished. Concerning the construction of the Nauvoo House, John Taylor wrote the following in his journal dated 18 August 1845:

> In council with Twelve and Bishops at President Brigham Young's. I also counselled with my brethren about sending two men, Brother's Samuel Bent and Charles C. Rich, in the counties around to collect subscriptions for the papers and the support of the press. This morn-

Nauvoo House–Riverside Mansion. Photograph courtesy of Harold Allen.

ing they commenced laying brick on the Nauvoo House. I was present when they commenced. Elder Kimball made a prayer on the occasion; there were a great number of bricklayers on hand ready to commence and all seemed to enjoy good spirits.[102]

On 2 October 1841, Joseph Smith placed the manuscript of the *Book of Mormon* in the southeast cornerstone. Ebenezer Robinson, a prominent citizen of Nauvoo, recalled the event:

> After the brethren had assembled at the southeast corner of the foundation, where the cornerstone was to be laid, President Joseph Smith said: "Wait, brethren, I have a document I wish to put in that stone," and started for his house, which was only a few rods away, across Main Street. I went with him to the house, and also one or two other brethren. He got a manuscript copy of the Book of Mormon, and brought it into the room where we were standing, and said: "I will examine to see if it is all here," and as he did so I stood near him, at his left side, and saw distinctly the writing, as he turned up the pages until he hastily went through the book and satisfied himself that it was all there. . . . It was written on foolscap paper, and formed a package, as the sheets lay flat, of about two or two and a half inches thick, I should judge. It was written mostly in Oliver Cowdery's handwriting, with which I was intimately acquainted, having set many pages of type from his handwriting, in the church printing office at Kirtland, Ohio. Some parts of it were written in other hand-

Nauvoo House Cornerstone. Photograph courtesy of Archives and Manuscripts, Harold B. Lee Library, B.Y.U.

writing. He took the manuscript and deposited it in the cornerstone of the Nauvoo House.[103]

After the Prophet Joseph's death the title of the Nauvoo House went to Emma Smith. Later, when Emma married Lewis Bidamon, he used the portions of the uncompleted structure to build a two-story house on the southwest corner of the original building. The completed structure was known as the Riverside Mansion.

In 1882, Mr. Bidamon uncovered the cornerstone. The following report was carried in the Carthage, Illinois *Republican* newspaper:

Last Tuesday, while Major Bidamon was tearing down the walls of the eastern wing of the old "Nauvoo House," . . . he came across the corner stone, which was laid by the Prophet the year 1841. The stone was in the foundation, in the southeast corner, and in the center of it was a square cut chest, about 10 x 14 inches, and eight inches deep, covered with a stone lid, which fitted closely in a groove or shoulder at the top, and cemented around the edge with lead that had been melted and poured in the seam. On removing the lid, which was done with some difficulty, the chest was found to be filled with a number of written and printed documents, the most of them mouldy and more or less decayed.[104]

Apparently, Mr. Bidamon gave pages of the *Book of Mormon* manuscript to different Nauvoo visitors.

\*

# 77. NAUVOO HOUSE DOCK AND STEAMBOAT LANDING

The Nauvoo House dock and steamboat landing was at the south end of Main Street.

### Historical Background

There were numerous boat and ferry landings in Nauvoo. Three important landings were the Kimball Landing, located at the west end of Hyrum Street, the Parley Landing at the end of Parley Street, and the Nauvoo House dock.

New converts from the East, Canada, and the British Isles arrived in the city regularly. The attitude of some of these converts can be understood from the words of William Clayton, an English convert who arrived for the first time in Nauvoo on 24 November 1840. Clayton recorded:

> We proceeded . . . to move our luggage to a new house on the banks of the Mississippi river. Thus ended a journey of over 5000 miles

Nauvoo House Dock. Photograph courtesy of LDS Historical Department.

having been exactly 11 weeks and about ten hours between leaving Liverpool and arriving at our journey's end . . . through the mercy of God we landed safe and in good health with the exception of eight persons one of whom died soon after landing.[105]

"We are pleased," Clayton continued, "to find ourselves once more at home, and felt to praise God for his goodness." Being with the Saints was for many being at home though they had never been to Nauvoo and in many cases were thousands of miles from their native land.

As more Saints arrived "home" to their Zion, many reunions of former friends and new Saints occurred at the boat landings at Nauvoo. On 27 March 1842 several thousand Saints gathered at the Mississippi River. In the distance they could see the ninety-five-ton *Ariel* steaming up the Mississippi. The deck was crowded with almost two hundred English converts who were not expecting such a welcome. As the little steamboat neared the landing, her passengers were singing a hymn above the noise of the throbbing engines. Joseph Smith, Willard Richards, Brigham Young, and William Clayton were among the crowd awaiting their arrival. The latter wept when he recognized friends from Manchester, where he had lived. Lyman Wright, leader of the emigrant company, reported to Joseph Smith that the Saints brought with them "about three thousand dollars worth of goods for the Temple and Nauvoo House."[106] After a round of handshaking, embraces, and tears, the emigrants were taken to various homes and settled for their first night in the City of the Saints.

The following extracts from the Prophet's journal mention a typical occurrence at the dock:

> Saturday, July 15th 1843 — At home 6 pm with my family and about one hundred others took a pleasure excursion on the Maid of Iowa from Nauvoo House Landing to the north part of the city and back at dusk. Theatre in the evening by Mr. Chapman. [107]
>
> Saturday 13 April 1844 — About 5 pm. the "Maid of Iowa" Steamer arrived at the Nauvoo House Wharf filled with passengers from England led by Elder William Kay. They started from Liverpool, 210 souls and nearly all arrived in good health and spirits.[108]

Another steamboat is mentioned by Heber C. Kimball:

> Tuesday 10 September 1844 — I was sick. Went to Brigham Young's. He and I went to the foot of Main Street. The Osprey landed there. Elder Hyde left for Ohio, Elder Rigdon left.[109]

A *Nauvoo Neighbor* advertisement dated 5 March 1845 illustrates the steamboats' busy scheduled service to Nauvoo:

ARRIVALS
Feb. 27, 1845 — Mermaid, going up
Feb. 28, 1845 — St. Croix, down
March 1, 1845 — Falchion, down
March 2, 1845 — Osprey, down
March 3, 1845 — Uncle Toby, down
March 3, 1845 — Sarah Ann, down

DEPARTURES
Feb. 28, 1845 — Lynx, going down
March 1, 1845 — New Haven, down
March 3, 1845 — Mermaid, down
March 4, 1845 — Osprey, down

One former citizen explained another use for the Nauvoo House dock during the winter season:

> In the coldness of the winter of 1842–1843 when the Mississippi was frozen over for several months. One freezing day Joseph Smith did not go to his office. Instead he remained at home to play with his children on the ice. They were sliding down the sloping lower end of Main Street near the Homestead where enough momentum could be gained to send the loaded sleigh out onto the smooth ice of the river. Joseph Smith III, Alexander, and Frederick G. were engaged in this activity. Soon other children gathered and the Prophet taught some of the older children how to slide on the soles of their shoes, balancing their bodies erectly. Others he taught how to steer the crude wooden sleighs of the day with their feet.[110]

☐

# 78.  THE JOSEPH SMITH HOMESTEAD

The Joseph Smith Homestead is near the southwest corner of Main and Water streets. Extant two-story log cabin and frame addition. Frame addition was built during Mormon period. Reconstructed log cabin (summer kitchen) on original site.

Joseph Smith homestead; cabin portion still visible. Photograph courtesy of LDS Historical Department.

Joseph Smith homestead. Photograph courtesy of LDS Historical Department.

## Historical Background

Originally used as the first Indian agency established in Illinois in 1803. This cabin was part of the first 135 acres of land purchased by the Church. Joseph and his wife Emma moved into the log cabin on 10 May 1839. The wooden frame addition was constructed in 1840.

Joseph Smith, Sr. log cabin. Photograph courtesy of the authors.

The Prophet lived here with his family until the Mansion House was completed in 1843, though the homestead was in continuous use for several years thereafter by the Smith family.

Joseph Smith III recalled his family's arrival at Commerce (Nauvoo) and the hiding places in the Homestead in his memoirs:

> [We] left Quincy, May 9, arrived at Commerce the following day, and moved into a log house. . . . Grandfather Joseph [and] Lucy Smith [lived in] a small log house on the west side of the frame attachment to the block house. . . . the Hugh White farm was a veritable plantation. There were the usual adjuncts [buildings]. . . . an addition was made to the back of the block house in which we lived. . . . Our house faced south, and this addition was to the north . . . . As for hiding places, there was, in this addition to the old building . . . a small hidden retreat . . . a little way down the stairway to the cellar the bearers of the steps were cut in two and the upper portion of the stairs furnished with hinges to allow that part to be lifted forward. This provided an entrance into the small retreat mentioned. It was a vaulted place, with a dry floor of brick and bricked walls, and was large enough for a couple of people to occupy, either sitting or lying down. . . . this small room was occupied a few times by Father when hunted, and was never, so far as I know, discovered by any of those who sought him, though the members of the family knew of its existence.[111]

O

## 79. THE SMITH FAMILY CEMETERY

The Smith family cemetery is on the Homestead property at Main and Water streets.

### Historical Background

Joseph Smith Sr. died on 14 September 1840 and was buried in the family cemetery. Several other Smith family members were buried here in the 1840s, including Don Carlos Smith who died on 7 August 1841 and Samuel Smith who died 30 July 1844, a few weeks following the assassination of his brothers, Joseph and Hyrum. After the murder of Joseph and Hyrum, their bodies were removed from

Emma Smith's grave (foreground) before reburial. Photograph courtesy of LDS Historical Department.

the outer pine boxes in which the Saints had viewed them before the public funeral in the Mansion House. Bags of sand replaced the bodies in the coffins, and were taken to the burial site at the temple. That evening about midnight, Dimick Huntington and several other men, directed by Emma, buried the bodies of the prophet and patriarch in the dirt basement of the uncompleted Nauvoo House to protect the bodies from mutilation by their enemies. A heavy rain in the night helped disguise the burial place from any would-be mobs.

Emma knew that this could be only a temporary location, since work on the Nauvoo House might disturb the graves. The decision was made to remove the bodies, again under the cover of darkness. Sometime around midnight, Emma had Gilbert Goldsmith, Jonathan Holmes, city coroner Dimick Huntington, and city sexton William Huntington remove the bodies from the Nauvoo House site across the street to the Homestead property. About twenty-five paces from the southeast corner of the Homestead stood the "spring house," a small shed. The men removed the shed and placed the bodies side by side in the new grave and then moved the shed back to its original spot. The exact location of the martyrs' graves was lost when Emma Smith died in 1879. RLDS Church leaders had the bodies of Joseph and Hyrum found, exhumed, and reburied on 20 January 1928. The graves of Joseph and Hyrum were marked for the first time. Lucy Mack, Don Carlos, Samuel, Emma, and Joseph Smith III's first wife, Emmeline Griswold, and two children are also buried here, on "God's Acre."

## O
## 80.   THE NAUVOO SURVEY STONE

The Nauvoo survey stone is at the southwest corner of Main and Water streets.

### Historical Background

In 1968, archaeologist J.C. Harrington confirmed that the original survey of 1839 was plotted true north and that every street, except Water Street, which followed the course of the river, ran parallel or at right angles to the survey line.[112]

The design of Nauvoo was greatly influenced by the plan for the "City of Zion" at Jackson County, Missouri. The first plan of Nauvoo

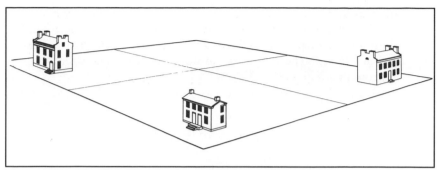

Nauvoo City Plat Plan. Drawing by and courtesy of Harold Allen.

was drawn on 30 August 1839 and included most of the 671 acres under Church ownership. The city plan, unlike the plan of Zion, provided for smaller blocks of four acres, each divided into four lots. The city was officially organized on 3 February 1841; and soon thereafter the new city council began passing ordinances on public works, building and land restrictions, and the beautification of the city.

Nauvoo was intended to have an open setting with sidewalks eight feet wide and streets almost fifty feet wide. Three larger streets — Main, Water, and Granger — would have wider sidewalks. Homes were to be set at a certain distance from the road, and trees and plants were to be incorporated as part of the landscape. Often the streets were surveyed and opened when enough people began to locate in an area. In this sense, most of Nauvoo was just a "paper" town in the fall of 1839; but by 1841, almost eighty percent of the original plat was opened. Sources indicate that some open roads were paved with gravel, and some sidewalks with brick, gravel, or stone.

The Saints in Nauvoo were unable to realize the ideal vision of the City Beautiful because of the unprecedented growth of the city. Lots were subdivided as new emigrants arrived in the city looking for places to live. The lack of funds to complete all the many building projects, both public and private, slowed the pace of opening new streets and additional areas in the city, and street improvements were often lacking. Nevertheless, the incredible effort of building the city with its temple during such a short space of time is one of the great stories of settlement in North America.

J.H. Buckingham, from Boston, visited Illinois in 1847, just after the Saints left Nauvoo, and reported his impressions of the abandoned city:

Time was, and that not two years and a half ago, when every house was full and every farm under cultivation, now, everything looks forlorn and desolate, not half the buildings are occupied, ... The stores are closed. The farms are running to waste. The streets are overgrown with grass.[113]

☐
# 81.   THE JOSEPH SMITH MANSION HOUSE

The Joseph Smith Mansion House is at the northeast corner of Main and Water streets. Extant two-story frame home. It originally had twenty-two rooms. Its roof, broad pilasters, and triple window are typical of late Federal homes of New England, yet some of the details are Greek Revival.

### Historical Background

Joseph Smith was born on 23 December 1805 at Sharon, Windsor County, Vermont. He married Emma Hale on 18 January 1827 at South Bainbridge, New York. Smith was baptized on 13 May 1829. He located in Commerce (Nauvoo), Illinois, in the summer of 1839. He was endowed in the upper floor of his General Store on 5 May 1842.

Emma Hale was born on 10 July 1804 at Harmony, Susquehannah County, Pennsylvania. She was baptized on 28 June 1830 at Colesville, New York. Emma was chosen the first president of the Nauvoo Female Relief Society on 17 March 1842. She was endowed in the upper floor of the Joseph Smith Mansion House on or before 28 September 1843. After Joseph's death, she remained in the Nauvoo area with her children and married Lewis C. Bidamon on 23 December 1847. She participated in the RLDS Church until her death on 30 April 1879.

Joseph moved his family into the Mansion House on or about 31 August 1843. He leased the hotel (retaining several rooms for his own family) to Ebenezer Robinson in January 1844 for one thousand dollars per annum. The Mansion House functioned as the Smith private residence, a hotel, and a meeting place for civic and church councils; and the upper east room served as a prayer room. The prophet recorded several events in his journal during this period:

Sunday, September 3rd 1843.    6 o'clock evening Joseph, Hyrum, W. Marsh, Newell K. Whitney, William Law and Miller in council at Joseph prayed for Hyrum's sick child and Whitney's etc.

Thursday, September 28th 1843   At 7 o'clock in the evening met at the Mansion's upper room front with William Law and William Marks. Joseph Smith was by common consent and unanimous voice chosen President of the quorum of the anointed and anointed and ordained to the highest and holiest order of the priesthood (and companion). Present: Joseph Smith, Hyrum Smith, George Miller, Newell K. Whitney, Willard Richards, John Smith, John Taylor, Amasa Lyman, Lucien Woodworth, John M. Bernhisel, William Law, William Marks. President Joseph led in prayer that his days might be prolonged, have dominion over his enemies, all the households be blessed and all the church and world.[114]

Tuesday, October 3rd, 1843.    At home. The brethren assembled with their wives to the amount of about one hundred couples and dined at the Nauvoo Mansion as an "opening" to the house. A very pleasant day and all things passed off well. In the evening Mr. William Backenstos was married to Miss Clara M. Wasson at the Mansion. I solemnized the marriage in presence of a select party.[115]

Joseph Smith Mansion House. Photograph courtesy of RLDS Graphic Design Commission.

The bodies of Joseph and Hyrum Smith were returned to Nauvoo the day following their deaths. A large procession met the wagons carrying the bodies of Joseph and Hyrum on Mulholland, east of town, and followed them to the Mansion House. On 29 June, Joseph's and Hyrum's bodies lay in state at the Mansion House from 8:00 A.M. until 5:00 P.M., allowing an estimated 20,000 Saints to view their fallen leaders before burial. Zina Jacobs recorded her experiences at the viewing on 28 June 1844:

> This afternoon the bodies of the martyrs arrived in town. . . . I went into his house for the first time and saw the lifeless, speechless bodies of the two martyrs for the testimony which they held. Little did my heart ever think that mine eyes should witness this awful scene.[116]

The widows of Joseph and Hyrum were devastated by news of the assassinations. Emma was five months pregnant at the time. The feelings and the emotional state of many Saints during this fateful period have been preserved in several extant letters and diaries. Vilate Kimball, wife of Apostle Heber C. Kimball, provided a detailed view of the confusion and intense emotional atmosphere following the martyrdom. In a letter dated 30 June 1844, Vilate wrote her husband who had been absent from Nauvoo during the month of June 1844:

> Never before, did I take up my pen to address you under so trying circumstances as we are now placed, but as Br Adams the bearer of this can tell you more than I can write I shall not attempt to describe the scene that we have passed through. God forbid that I should ever witness another like unto it. I saw the lifeless corpses of our beloved brethren when they were brought to their almost distracted families. Yea I witnessed their tears, and groans, which was enough to rent the heart of an adamant. Every brother and sister that witnessed the scene felt deeply to sympathize with them. Yea, every heart is filled with sorrow, and the very streets of Nauvoo seem to mourn. Where it will end the Lord only knows. We are kept awake night after night by the alarm of mobs.[117]

O

# 82. THE SIDNEY RIGDON HOME AND POST OFFICE

The Sidney Rigdon home is on the east side of Main between Water and Sidney streets. Extant two-story frame home with post-Mormon addition.

### Historical Background

Sidney Rigdon was born on 19 February 1793 at St. Clair, Allegheny County, Pennsylvania. He married Phebe Brook on 12 June 1820. Rigdon was baptized on 15 November 1830 at Kirtland, Ohio. He became a member of the Church's First Presidency on 18 March 1833. He arrived in Commerce with his family in 1839. He served as city postmaster, and his home was the post office in Nauvoo. He was endowed on 11 May 1844. Rigdon was the President of the Church of Christ (a post-Nauvoo church), which he organized on 7 and 8 April 1845 near Pittsburgh, Pennsylvania.

Many issues of Nauvoo newspapers carried lists informing individuals that they had unclaimed letters at the post office:

Sidney Rigdon home. Photograph courtesy of Harold Allen.

A List of Letters

Remaining in the Post Office at Nauvoo, Hancock County, Illinois. April 1. 1843 which if not taken out before the first of July next, will be sent the Post Office Department as dead letters.

Any person calling for any of the following letters will please say they are advertized or they may not get them. [Over one hundred names were listed, including Joseph Smith, Brigham Young, Luana Rockwell, Elizabeth Knight, Sylvester Stoddard, Edwin Webb, and Hyrum Smith.][118]

A description of the Nauvoo post office is in Charlotte Haven's letter to her parents, dated 5 March 1843:

> We enter a side door leading into the kitchen, and in a corner near the door is a wide shelf or table, on which against the wall is a sort of cupboard with pigeon-holes or boxes. This is the post office. In this room, with the great cooking stove at one end, the family eats and sits. Mrs. Rigdon when I go for the mail always invites me to stop and rest, which after a cold long walk I am glad to do.[119]

O

# 83.  THE SOUTH WING OF AN EARLY HOTEL

The south wing of an early Nauvoo hotel is at the northwest corner of Main and Sidney streets. Extant two-story frame building. Federal style with New England influence such as triple windows and horizontal siding.

## Historical Background

This was one of the earliest hotels in the city of Nauvoo and was referred to as the City Hotel, Mills Hotel, and Masonic Tavern.

An incident between two young men in front of the Mills City Hotel caught the attention of Joseph Smith, who was in session with the city council at the Red Brick Store. Joseph was presiding when he noticed through the window the two young men. One of the young men recalled that Joseph came running out of the store and "vaulted over a fence, and ran diagonally northeast toward us and arrived just

Early Hotel. Photograph courtesy of LDS Historical Department.

as we had pulled pickets from a fence and were about to continue our quarrel with the pickets."[120] The prophet's journal picks up the story:

> While the court was in session 2 boys were seen fighting in the street by Mill's tavern. [I] saw it and ran over immediately, caught one of the boys (who had begun the fight with clubs) and stopped him and then the other. [I] gave the bystanders a lecture for not interfering in such cases and returned to court. [I told the boys] "Nobody is allowed to fight in this city but me."[121]

\*

## 84.  THE DANIEL BUTLER HOME AND COBBLER SHOP FOUNDATION

The Daniel Butler home and cobbler shop was built on the north side of Parley between Main and Hyde streets. Nonextant two-story brick home. Notice in the photo the attempt to conceal the roof with the extended facade of the end wall.

Daniel Butler home. Photograph courtesy of LDS Historical Department.

### Historical Background
Daniel Butler was born on 13 April 1802 at New Bedford, Bristol County, Massachusetts. Butler's shop was probably more like a general store than exclusively a cobbler shop.

O

## 85.   THE SIMEON DUNN HOME

The Simeon Dunn home is at the southwest corner of Parley and Hyde streets. Extant two-story brick home.

### Historical Background
Simeon Dunn was born on 7 August 1804 in Williamstown, Ontario County, New York. He married Adeline Rawson on 3 July 1828. Dunn was baptized on 15 April 1839 at Van Buren, Missouri.

Simeon Dunn home. Photograph courtesy of RLDS Graphic Design Commission.

He made a brief visit to Nauvoo on 20 June 1840 and moved his family to Nauvoo on 5 August 1841. He was chosen as the senior president of the Fifteenth Quorum of Seventies in 1844, and was endowed in the Nauvoo Temple on 20 December 1845.

Simeon Dunn recorded the following:

> We arrived in Nauvoo August 5, 1841, settled in that city. . . . In September 1841, I was sent on a mission to West Canada to preach the gospel. I was ordained one of the seventies [in Nauvoo] under the hands of Levi Hancock. In May 1844, I was sent on a mission to the state of New York. On January 26, 1845, I was ordained and set apart to be the senior president of the fifteenth Quorum of Seventy. . . . On May 18, I left Nauvoo to follow in [the] wake and share in all the toils and suffering of the Saints.[122]

○

# 86.   THE HENRY THOMAS HOME

The Henry Thomas home is on the east side of Hyde between Parley and Sidney streets. Extant two-story brick home.

### Historical Background

Henry Thomas was born on 27 December 1781 near Rockingham, Richmond County, North Carolina. He married Ester Thomas in 1808. Thomas was baptized on 9 June 1836. He was endowed in the Nauvoo Temple on 20 January 1846.

Henry Thomas home. Photograph courtesy of the authors.

O

## 87.  THE HIRAM CLARK HOME

The Hiram Clark home is at the southwest corner of Hyde and Sidney streets. Extant two-story brick home.

### Historical Background

Hiram Clark was born on 22 September 1795 at Wells, Rutland County, Vermont. He married Mary Fenno. Clark was baptized on 22 March 1835. He arrived in Nauvoo in March 1839. He bought this homesite for $500 and began construction in the spring or summer of 1843. He was a member of the Nauvoo Legion.

Hiram Clark home. Photograph courtesy of the authors.

*

# 88.   THE THEODORE TURLEY HOME SITE

The Theodore Turley home site is on the west side of Hyde between Sidney and Water streets.

### Historical Background

Theodore Turley was born on 10 April 1801 at Birmingham, Warwickshire, England. He married Frances A. Kimberley on 26 November 1821. Turley was baptized on 1 March 1837 at Ontario, Canada. Turley arrived at Commerce (Nauvoo) in 1839. He built a log cabin at this site sometime in 1839 and it is purported to be the first home built by the Mormons at Nauvoo. He was a member of the Nauvoo Legion and was endowed in the Nauvoo Temple on 20 December 1845.

Turley reported in his diary on 21 September 1839 the following description of his situation following his arrival in Commerce (Nauvoo):

> Took leave of my family this day under peculiar circumstances considering the late troubles we have had in the State of Missouri. . . . journeying with my wife and six children two hundred miles in a weeks time, living in a tent for the space of thirteen weeks and never having the privilege of sleeping under a roof for this time. When we arrived in Commerce in the Spring of 1839 it being a new place on the banks of the Great Mississippi River hence without a house or convenience of a house to shelter in, but spring being advanced it [was] necessary to start planting some corn and potatoes etc., before I started to build my house . . . I began to get logs, [and] stone.[123]

# Outskirts
## and Additional Photographs

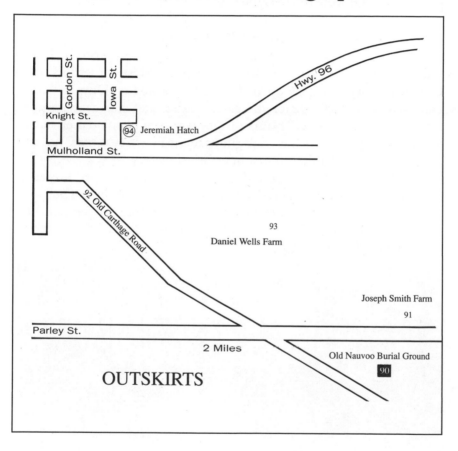

*

# 90.   OLD NAUVOO BURIAL GROUND

The Old Nauvoo Burial Ground is two miles east from Durphy (Hwy 96) on the south side of Parley Street.

### Historical Background

There are several burial sites in and around Nauvoo, including Indian burial grounds, private lots used by pre-Mormon settlers, and a Commerce city cemetery opened in 1839 (located on Durphy Street) and used until 1847. After the exodus, the new city center moved from the Flats to "Upper" Nauvoo. The people of Nauvoo then moved the cemetery because it was contiguous to the new city center. In 1848, the bodies were re-interred in a new city cemetery.[124]

During the Mormon period, several individuals were buried in their families' city lots, especially small infants and children. The Smith family buried many of their relatives at the Homestead property, including Joseph and Lucy Mack Smith and their sons Samuel, Don Carlos, Hyrum, and Joseph.

Old Nauvoo Burial Ground. Photograph courtesy of LDS Historical Department.

In 1842 the Saints opened a new cemetery southeast of the city, now known as the Old Pioneer Cemetery. The following advertisement appeared in the *Wasp* newspaper on 4 June 1842. "The burying Ground southeast of the city has been laid out in family burying lots. A number of which will be offered for sale."[125]

Charles Lambert, a Nauvoo Temple stonecutter, relates the following about the Old Nauvoo Burial Ground:

> I must mention a circumstance that took place a short time previous to finishing the Temple. I was going home when my wife met me at the door and began crying—said she could stand anything but this (that was the children crying for bread and she had none to give them). I replied: Why do you not go and ask the Lord to send you some? Why not you go with me? We went into our bedroom and fastened ourselves in, and there made our request. In about an hour after, Brother Lucius Scovil came and after some little talk said he would like me to make a grave stone to mark the place where his son was buried. I told him I would do it. He said he was in no hurry but wanted it done. I told him I had a family depending on me. He said he did not have anything to pay with, but in a while told me he could let me have some wheat if I wished it. I told him I would be pleased to get some. He wished me to go with him and he would let me have it. I went got the wheat—4 or 4 1/2 bushels. I got it, took it to Knights' mill and returned home with the grist, thus were our prayers answered.[126]

*

# 91.  THE JOSEPH SMITH FARM SITE

The Joseph Smith farm was on the north side of Parley just beyond the Old Nauvoo Burial Ground.

### Historical Background
Joseph Smith purchased the farm property but was unable to manage the farm after 1842 because of the many responsibilities he had in Nauvoo. That same year he asked Cornelius Lott to manage the property for him. At one period the farm consisted of one-half section of fenced prairie land and a large home. Cornelius Lott and his wife,

Permelia D. Lott, spent much of their time breaking up the prairie land for cultivation.

Cornelius P. Lott was born on 27 September 1798 at New York City, New York County, New York. He married Permelia Darrow on 27 April 1823 at New York, New York. Lott was baptized before 1834 at Luzerne County, Pennsylvania. He was endowed on 9 December 1843, and again in the Nauvoo Temple on 11 December 1845.

Joseph and Hyrum were on their way to Carthage with several associates on 24 June 1844. As he passed by his farm on the old Carthage Road just outside the city, he stopped for a long period to admire it. As the company proceeded, Joseph hesitated several times, looking back at the farm. This hesitation caused several individuals to make remarks about his action, but Joseph replied: "If some of you had such a farm, and knew you would not see it any more, you would want to take a good look at it for the last time."[127]

*

## 92.   THE ROAD TO CARTHAGE

The road to Carthage begins in "upper" Nauvoo taking an approximate course to the Joseph Smith farm, except that the road ran about a quarter of a mile south. Near the Smith farm, the road veered southeast in a straight course to Carthage.

### Historical Background
In 1843 the Saints in Nauvoo produced a map of Hancock County. This map identifies the various roads and trails in the county. The Nauvoo–Carthage Road, a dirt road, has been marked and designated an "Historic Trail," and can be traveled.

*

## 93.   THE DANIEL WELLS HOME AND FARM SITE

The Daniel Wells home was built on his farm near the center of White

Traditionally identified as the Daniel H. Wells home. Photograph courtesy of LDS Historical Department.

Street, about 2366 North and 734 East. Nonextant two-story log home with smaller log wing and later brick structure attached.

### Historical Background

Daniel H. Wells was born on 27 October 1814 at Trenton, Oneida County, New York. He married Eliza Rebecca Robinson on 12 March 1837 at Commerce (Nauvoo). Wells was baptized on 9 August 1846 at Nauvoo. He moved to Commerce (Nauvoo) in 1834. Wells was not at that time a Church member, but was highly respected by the Saints. He was elected alderman and appointed a regent of the university as well as an officer in the Nauvoo Legion. He participated in the Battle of Nauvoo in September 1846. Wells was a member of the LDS Church First Presidency with Brigham Young in Salt Lake City, Utah.

The following account relates a last visit the Prophet Joseph Smith had with Wells at the Wells' residence:

> As [Joseph] passed out of the city, he called on Daniel H. Wells, Esq., who was unwell and on parting he said, "Squire Wells, I wish you to cherish my memory, and not think me the worst man in the world either."[128]

O

## 94.  THE JEREMIAH HATCH HOME

The Jeremiah Hatch home is at the southeast corner of Knight and Iowa (James) streets. Extant two-story brick home.

Jeremiah Hatch home. Photograph courtesy of the authors.

### Historical Background

Jeremiah Hatch was born on 23 September 1766 at Oblang, Dutchess County, New York. He married Elizabeth Haight on 23 November 1789 at Ferrisburg, Vermont. Hatch was baptized in 1840. He was endowed in the Nauvoo Temple on 21 January 1846.

The following photographs of historic Nauvoo homes are included, although the structures no longer exist nor has their exact location been determined. Some have been traditionally associated with various people; all help augment our appreciation of old Nauvoo.

Parley Street scene. Photograph courtesy of Robert Flanders.

Traditionally identified as the Frank Pullin home. Photograph courtesy of LDS Historical Department.

Thomas Pitt home. Photograph courtesy of LDS Historical Department.

Traditionally identified as the James Holt home. Photograph courtesy of LDS Historical Department.

Traditionally identified as the Charles Hooper home. Photograph courtesy of LDS Historical Department.

Nauvoo; unidentified. Photograph courtesy of Archives and Manuscripts, Harold B. Lee Library, B.Y.U.

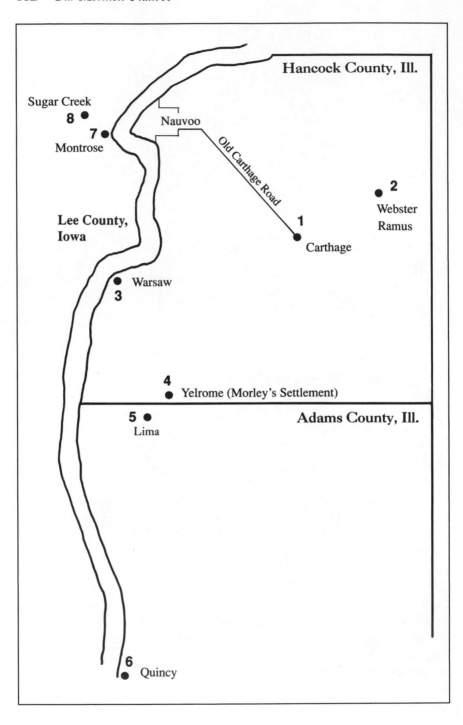

Hancock County, Ill.

Sugar Creek

**8** ●

**7**● Nauvoo

Montrose

Lee County,
Iowa

**2**
●
Webster
Ramus

Old Carthage Road

**1**

Carthage

● Warsaw

**3**

**4**
● Yelrome (Morley's Settlement)

**5** ●
Lima

Adams County, Ill.

**6**
● Quincy

# GUIDED TOURS OF
# THE SURROUNDING
# COMMUNITIES

The major settlements near Nauvoo were Montrose, Lee County, Iowa; Ramus, Hancock County, Illinois; and Lima, Adams County, Illinois. There were other small Mormon communities at Plymouth, Green Plains, and Golden's Point; and a Mormon presence was found in several non-Mormon communities such as Quincy, Carthage, Bear Creek, La Harpe, and Fountain Green. Nauvoo itself was surrounded by several "suburbs" such as Davis Mound, Mormon Springs, Rocky Run, and Sonora. Near the town of Warsaw, south of Nauvoo on the Mississippi River, a proposed Mormon settlement called Warren was planned.

When Joseph arrived in Illinois there were eighteen branches (congregations) of the Church; by 1845 there were thirty-four branches. This growth resulted principally because of the success of the British Mission and the creation of Mormon settlements in Iowa and Illinois.

The Nauvoo Stake (similar to a diocese) was organized on 5 October 1839. In 1840, six other stakes were organized in the area: Crooked Creek, later known as Ramus (Webster) on 4 July; Lima on 22 October; Quincy on 25 October; Mount Hope and Freedom on 27 October; Geneva on 1 November; and Springfield on 5 November. In time, Joseph dissolved these stakes in an effort to draw to Nauvoo the resources and individuals needed to build the temple. The branches remained intact until violence forced Saints in these stakes to move to Nauvoo for protection.

For the most part, the Saints were able to build their city without much opposition, although the expected problems between "old settlers" and "new settlers" were always present and some religious animosity was evident from the beginning. For example, a group of Protestant ministers burned the *Book of Mormon* in 1840;[1] however, open antagonism did not surface around Nauvoo until a few years later.

Dissension within the Church also contributed to hostile feelings between the Saints and their neighbors. A major cause of dissension was the excommunication of John C. Bennett. Several unscrupulous opportunists came to Nauvoo during this period; Bennett was one of them. He was so influential in helping the Saints obtain the Nauvoo city charter that he was voted the first mayor. Involvement in sexual misconduct forced him to resign from the office on 17 May 1842. After his expulsion from civic and religious offices in Nauvoo, the *Sangamo Journal* asked Bennett to write a series of articles critical of the Church in Nauvoo. His series of letters appeared in issues of the *Journal* from the first of July to September 1842. Bennett also lectured against the Church and published *The History of the Saints; or, An Expose' of Joe Smith and Mormonism.* He and other embittered dissenters attempted to raise feelings against the prophet and the Church.

Some of the non-Mormons in Hancock County were already worried about the economic and political power of the city of Nauvoo, and Bennett's charges seemed to validate their concerns. Religious and political differences sparked a campaign of harassment. The persecution had now begun in Illinois.

There were always individuals and communities who treated the Saints with generosity and kindness. From their initial expulsion from Missouri in 1838–1839 to their removal from Illinois in 1846, many people in the United States believed that the Saints had been wronged and that they deserved assistance from the community and nation at large.[2] However, there were not enough of those tolerant people in Hancock County to diffuse the volatile anti-Mormon sentiment.

In early 1844, bolder attacks against the Church, and actions to quell the dissent, pushed both the rhetoric and the strategies of the anti-Mormon movement beyond the possibility of peaceful compromise. After Joseph and Hyrum Smith were killed, there was a brief lull in direct confrontations between the Mormons and non-Mormons in Hancock County. The uneasy peace was short-lived. The Mormons' situation became increasingly unsettled in 1845 and early 1846. The Nauvoo city charter was revoked by the Illinois state legislature on 24 January 1845. This act left the city without a judicial system, a city government, a militia, or any significant legal protection from the mobs in Hancock County. It was at this time that the Mormons voted to re-name Nauvoo the City of Joseph. There was an increase of mob violence against outlying Mormon settlements, including those in Iowa. Nauvoo itself was endangered by threats from a large vigilante movement in the county. The situation worsened almost to the point of civil war.

During the fall of 1845, Church officials made an agreement with a commission from the state of Illinois that the Mormons would leave the following spring. As a result of mob pressure, the Twelve Apostles met on 24 September 1845 to draft a statement of their intention to leave the state:

> We, the undersigned members of a Council of the Church of Jesus Christ of Latter Day Saints assembled at the house of John Taylor, in the city of Nauvoo on the evening of the twenty-fourth day of September 1845, do hereby express our determination, to remove, in connection with as many of the members of the Church as will harken to our advise on the subject from this county and state as soon as property can be disposed of, and the necessary preparations made . . . as early as next spring, in April or May. . . . As we wish for peace, at any sacrifice which is in our power to make consistent with honor and virtue.[3]

The leaders in Nauvoo wanted to avoid the problems that they had encountered earlier in Missouri. If property could be disposed of at some price, and enough time given to prepare, many of the hardships encountered in 1838–1839 might be avoided.

To assist in this matter, the Nauvoo stake high council published a circular and sent it to several newspapers in the region on 20 January 1846. The purpose was to advertise the commitment of the Saints to leave Nauvoo and create interest in the various properties that were for sale in Nauvoo.

> Much of our property will be left in the hands of competent agents for sale at a low rate, for teams, for goods, and for cash. . . . we agreed to leave the country for the sake of peace, upon the condition that no more vexations, prosecutions be instituted against us. . . . in good faith have we labored to fulfill this engagement and such editors as are willing that we should live and not die . . . are respectfully requested to publish this article. And men who wish to buy property very cheap, to benefit themselves . . . are invited to call and look.[4]

Nevertheless, mob activity continued unabated to keep pressure on the Church. An advance company of Saints left Nauvoo under the leadership of Brigham Young in February 1846, crossing the Mississippi on rafts and flatboats. Later the river froze, and teams of oxen pulled wagons across the ice to Iowa.

Quincy and Fort Des Moines had served as refuges for the Saints fleeing Missouri. Sugar Creek now provided temporary safety for those leaving Nauvoo. Although some of the smaller surrounding communities of Nauvoo are not well known, they were settled with the same devotion, and left with the same reluctance.

# 1.   Carthage, Hancock County, Illinois

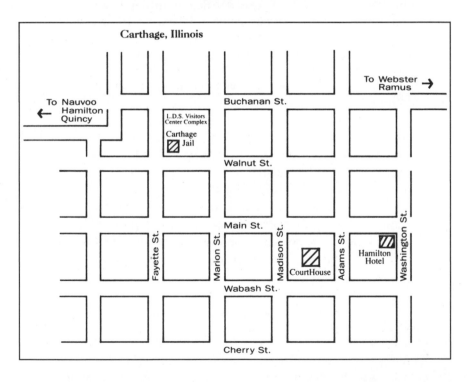

Carthage, Illinois is approximately 23 miles southeast of Nauvoo. Head south from Nauvoo on Highway 96 approximately 12 miles to Hamilton. At Hamilton take Highway 136 east for 11 miles.

The events of June 1844 gave the Carthage Jail, the Courthouse, and the Hamilton House national fame.

**Carthage Jail** is at the southwest corner of the intersection of Walnut and Marion streets.

**The County Courthouse site** is on the Public Square, which is bounded by Main Street on the north, Madison Street on the west, Wabash Street on the south, and Adams Street on the east.

**The Hamilton House site** is at the northeast corner of the intersection of Main and Washington streets.

## Historical Background

Carthage became the Hancock County seat before the Mormons arrived in Illinois. Between 1839–1846 Carthage had only a few hundred inhabitants, except during the few weeks each year that the circuit court was in session. During the two-week sessions beginning the third Mondays of May and October, Carthage was filled with hundreds of people who found their beds anywhere they could: in barns, in haystacks, and in wagons.

Three buildings were important during the Mormon period: the Carthage Jail, where Joseph Smith was killed; the County Courthouse, where Joseph was taken to answer the complaint of treason and where some of his murderers were tried; and the Hamilton House, a local hotel and tavern where the bodies of Joseph and Hyrum were taken after the assassinations.

**Carthage Jail**. For the first decade of the county's existence there was no county jail. On 9 July 1839, the Hancock County Commissioner's Court contracted with William Metcalf and Samuel Dickenson to build a jail in Carthage. They built this yellow limestone structure during 1840–1841 at a cost of $4,105. To provide a secure area, the foundation was made three feet thick and three feet deep. The walls of the jail are two-and-a-half feet thick at the first level and two feet thick at the second level. The interior of the jail originally consisted of seven separate rooms, including the living quarters for the jailor and his family, a debtors' cell, and a larger cell on the second level.

In 1844, several prominent defectors from the Church, under the direction of William Law, brought complaints against Nauvoo city officials, including Mayor Joseph Smith, for the destruction of the *Nauvoo Expositor*. With assurances of safety from Governor Thomas Ford, Smith and other leaders turned themselves over to county author-

Carthage Jail. Photograph courtesy of LDS Historical Department.

ities and proceeded to Carthage. Willard Richards, Joseph's private secretary, kept a detailed record:

> [June] 24 6:30 am   Started for Carthage [after] 10 miles arrived at Fellers. 4 miles from Carthage met Captain Dunn with an order from Governor Ford . . . Joseph countersigned the order and returned with all the company to Nauvoo. . . . moved to Carthage same day starting from Nauvoo about 6 pm and arrived at Carthage about fifteen to 12 midnight. [At] Fellers, 4 miles west of Carthage, Captain Dunn and his company of dragoons arrived and escorted us into Carthage.

At the same time, Thomas Sharp and others conspired with law-enforcement officers to take advantage of the arrests. Through legal maneuvers they managed to have the Mormon leaders illegally detained, giving them time to prepare for the assassination of the Smith brothers. Although the Governor pledged protection, the Mormons were apprehensive:

> [June] 25 . . . while in conversation, Constable Bettisworth arrested Joseph Smith for treason on complaint of Augustin Spencer. Hyrum was arrested for treason on complaint of H.O. Norton. 9:15 am Governor come and invited Joseph to walk. . . . [9 pm] Capt. Dunn escorted Joseph, Hyrum, Willard Richards, J.P. Green, Stephen Markham, Dan Jones, Dr. Southwick, Lorenzo Wasson, and John

Taylor to jail. We were received by the jailor, Mr Stigell, and first put in the criminals cell, but he afterward gave us the debtors department where we all slept from 11:30 till 6 am.

June 26th 1844. 7:00 am   Joseph and Hyrum ate with Stigell . . . Joseph sent word to his counsel by messengers that he wanted a change of venue. . . . 10:15 am [the] Governor left after saying that the prisoners were under his protection and probably they would go to Nauvoo . . . Joseph said I have had a good deal of anxiety about my safety, which I never did before, I could not help. . . . 3:40 pm taken by Constable Bettisworth from jail by a guard contrary to our wishes, compulsory and escorted to the courtroom [at] 4 o'clock. Case called by Robert F. Smith, J.P. Council called for subpoena. [At] 4:25 pm took copy of order to bring prisoners from jail for trial . . . [no trial] 5:30 returned to jail and Joseph and Hyrum thrust into close confinement . . . . Dr. Bernhisel brought the following, "I would advise the jailor to keep the Messrs. Smiths in the room in which I found them this morning, unless a closer confinement should be clearly necessary to prevent an escape." [signed] June 26, 1844 Thomas Ford

Governor and officers held a council and decided [that] the Governor and troops [should] go to Nauvoo tomorrow and return next day, leaving 50 men to guard the prisoners . . . Wood, Reid, and Green retired to Hamiltons' [hotel] and [at] 9:15 pm Elder Taylor prayed. John S. Fullmer, Taylor, Markham, Jones, and Richards stayed with Joseph and Hyrum in the front room.

As their confinement lengthened, Joseph and his followers busied themselves with the ordinary:

Thursday 27 June 1844   jail 5 am Phelps and Green called on their way to Nauvoo. 5:30 am breakfast . . . 8:20 am [Joseph] wrote Emma. . . . 1:15 pm Joseph, Hyrum and Willard dined in their room and Markham and Taylor [dined] below. [At] 1:30 pm Markham went . . . 3:15 pm the guards have been more severe in their operations, threatening among themselves . . . Taylor sung "Poor Way Faring Man of Grief." Hyrum read from Josephus. [At] 4 o'clock changed guard. [At] 4:15 pm Joseph commenced conversing with the guard.

Soon those confined would have their activities interrupted, and their loyalties tested:

Stigall [the jailor] returned from town and said Markham was surrounded by a mob and had gone to Nauvoo. [Stigall] suggested that they [Joseph and Hyrum] would be safer in the jail. Joseph said, "after supper we will go in." Stigall went out and Joseph said to Dr. Richards, "If we go in the jail will you go in with us." Dr. answered, "Bro. Joseph, you did not ask me to cross the river with you, you did not ask me to come to Carthage, you did not ask me to come to jail with you, and do you think I would forsake you now? But I will tell you what I will do, if you are condemned to be hung for treason I will be hung in your stead and you shall go free." Joseph [said] "you cannot." Dr. said, "I will" . . . the guard turned to go out [and] when at the stairs top, some one below called him 2 or 3 times. He went down, a little rustling at the door [and] the cry surrender and [the] discharge of 3 or 4 arms followed instantly. Dr. glanced an eye by the curtain [and] saw a 100 armed men around the door. Joseph, Hyrum, and Taylor coats were off. Joseph [reached] for Mortons' cane. Dr. for Taylors' cane. All [of us] sprang against the door. The balls whistled up the stairway and in an instant one came through the door. Joseph, Taylor, and Richards sprang to the left and Hyrum back in front of the door. [He] snapped his pistol, when a ball struck him in the left side of his nose. [He] fell back on floor saying, "*I am a dead man.*" Joseph discharged his 6 shooter in the entry reaching round the door casing. Discharges continued [to] come in the room. 6 shooter missed fired 2 or 3 times. Taylor sprang to leap from the east window [and] was shot in the window.[5]

Then Joseph went to the window. The mob outside fired at him from below as he was struck by bullets fired from inside the jail. He fell through the window, exclaiming, "Oh Lord my God."

Non-Mormon eyewitnesses said Joseph was not dead when he fell: "He raised himself up against the well curb . . . drew up one leg and stretched out the other and died immediately."[6]

Apostle John Taylor was wounded in the attack, but Richards was unharmed. He tended Taylor's injuries, then cared for the bodies of Joseph and Hyrum. An examination of Joseph's body showed that four bullets had struck him: one in the right collar bone, one in the breast, and two in the back.

It was then Richards' duty to send word to Nauvoo:

> Carthage Jail, 8 o'clock, 5 min., p.m. June 27th, 1844. Joseph and Hyrum are dead. Taylor wounded, not very badly. I am well. Our guard was forced, as we believe, by a band of Missourians from 100 to 200. The job was done in an instant, and the party fled towards Nauvoo instantly. This is as I believe it. The citizens here are afraid of the "Mormons" attacking them; I promised them no. [signed] Willard Richards

N.B. — The citizens promise us protection; alarm guns have been fired. [signed] John Taylor[7]

**County Courthouse.** The first courthouse in Hancock County was a log structure built in 1833. In 1839 Moses Stephens built a second courthouse on the site of the present county courthouse on Main Street near the Hamilton Hotel. The Stephens courthouse, razed in 1906, was a two-story brick building. The first floor consisted of four rooms which served as offices for the county sheriff, treasurer, the clerks of the circuit court, and the county commissioners' court. A large courtroom and two jury rooms were located on the second floor.

On 19 May 1845 another court term began in Carthage, and included the trial of those accused of the murders of Joseph and Hyrum Smith. The second floor courtroom was filled to capacity from the first hour of the opening day of testimony.

Carthage Courthouse. Photograph courtesy of LDS Historical Department.

On Friday, 30 May, Judge Richard Young instructed the jury and then adjourned the court for lunch. The jury was escorted to their room for deliberation. At two o'clock the court reconvened. The jury had reached a verdict, "[We] find the defendants *Not Guilty* as charged in this indictment."[8]

Brigham Young noted in his journal that the defendants had been acquitted "as we had anticipated."[9] Though several local Hancock County papers justified the mob action against the Smith brothers, other papers in Illinois and throughout the United States saw the assassination of the prophet and patriarch as a sign that mob rule was a disease spreading across the nation. Many of these papers regarded Joseph Smith as an imposter; nevertheless, as reported in the *Hampshire Gazette*, they "deplored the manner and circumstances of his death, as eminently wicked, disgraceful, and dangerous in their tendencies."[10]

**Hamilton House Site**. The Hamilton Tavern, commonly known as the Hamilton House, was owned and operated by Artois Hamilton. Joseph, Hyrum, and Governor Ford were all at the Hamilton House a few nights before the killings. The bodies of Joseph and Hyrum were taken there the evening of June 27. Rough coffins were made and the bodies were placed inside.

The next day Artois Hamilton and Samuel Smith (a brother of Joseph and Hyrum) took the bodies in two separate wagons back to Nauvoo where the Saints awaited their prophet and their patriarch.

Hamilton House. Photograph courtesy of LDS Historical Department.

# 2. Webster (Ramus), Hancock County, Illinois

Webster, also known as Ramus or Macedonia during the Mormon period, is northeast of Carthage. Take Highway 136 east from Carthage for about 6 miles. Go north (a left turn) at the Webster/Fountain Green turn off (2500 East); drive north about 4.5 miles. This is the site of Webster.

**The old Webster cemetery** is west of the city center. Turn north (left) at 2610 East and follow this road for about 1/4 mile. Joseph Smith's sister, Catherine Salisbury, is buried there.

**The Webster Community Church**, purportedly built on the foundation of the first Mormon chapel, is southeast of the city center.

### Historical Background

Ramus, a Latin word, means "branch." Members of the Church who lived near Crooked Creek laid out this small community under the direction of Joel Johnson. Johnson had settled near Crooked Creek and converted several other families to the Church. He was called to be the stake president when it was organized on 15 July 1840.

Ramus Cemetery. Photograph courtesy of the authors.

During the Mormon period a road to Ramus connected with a road to Carthage, making it convenient for Joseph to visit friends and family there. Joseph's sisters Sophronia and Catherine lived in this Mormon settlement. Catherine died in her home near Ramus on 1 February 1900.

The Ramus Saints built an early meeting house, an unusual practice for the time. The local church in Webster is purported to be built upon its foundation.

The Prophet Joseph Smith attended several meetings which were held in Ramus. Sections 130 and 131 of the LDS *Doctrine and Covenants* are extracts taken from William Clayton's diary (at the time Joseph's secretary).[11] These excerpts were later included in Joseph's personal diary.

Joseph prophesied at Ramus on 2 April 1843 — a prophecy many believe to accurately foretell the commencement of the American Civil War:

> I prophecy in the Name of the Lord God that the commencement of bloodshed as preparatory to the coming of the Son of Man will commence in South Carolina. (It probably may come through the slave trade) This the voice declared to me while I was praying earnestly on the subject 25 December 1832.[12]

# 3.  Warsaw, Hancock County, Illinois

Warsaw is about 15 miles south of Nauvoo. Take Highway 96 south from Nauvoo through Hamilton to the Warsaw Road. Then take the Warsaw Road southwest for about 3.5 miles to the Warsaw city center. Warsaw Road becomes Main Street in Warsaw.

**The Warsaw House Hotel**, also known as Flemming's Tavern, is located at 130 Main Street. The brick portion of this building was the original Warsaw Hotel where the murderers of Joseph and Hyrum Smith assembled following the assassination.

**Thomas Sharp's** *Warsaw Signal* office, a brick building east of the Warsaw Hotel, was probably at 204 Main Street.

Main Street, Warsaw, (Sharp's *Warsaw Signal* Office). Photograph courtesy of Library of Congress.

## Historical Background

Warsaw was a community of about five hundred people during the 1840s. It was here that the Anti-Mormon Party was founded in 1841 by Thomas Sharp to counter the growing Mormon political power in Hancock County and in the state. (In contemporary diaries and letters they are called Anties.) Sharp was the editor of the influential *Warsaw Signal*, a leading anti-Mormon newspaper.

Sharp reportedly stated on the evening of 27 June 1844, "We have finished the leading men of the Mormon Church."[13] Participants in the murders of Joseph and Hyrum assembled after the assassination at the Warsaw House, Mrs. Flemming's tavern. Some sixty men arrived later for supper, openly rejoicing, bragging about killing the Smith brothers that day.

The *Warsaw Signal* defended the killing of the Smith brothers. Sharp wrote that because of the Mormon leaders' "outrages on the rights of our citizens," the killing of the Smiths, which was done by our "most respectable citizens, [was justified and] that the act ought to be done and that the perpetrators would not only be protected but honored."[14]

Even after Joseph's death the Church continued to grow both numerically and politically. However, the anti-Mormon resentment

Flemming Tavern. Photograph courtesy of the authors.

did not subside. The *Warsaw Signal* continued to print articles denouncing the Mormons. "The people of Hancock never can be at rest until Nauvoo is made desolate,"[15] wrote Thomas Sharp. This hostility towards the Mormons continued until they left Nauvoo in 1846.

# 4. Morley's Settlement, Hancock County, Illinois

Morley's Settlement is 25 miles south of Nauvoo. Take Highway 96 south toward Quincy. Approximately 10 miles from the Warsaw Road (about 2.5 miles before Lima) is the road to Tioga. Turn east (left) and travel 1.5 miles east (this turn-off road becomes 80 North in Tioga). Turn south (right) at the stop sign at 840 East. Head south about 1 mile to where the road forks. This is the site of Morley's Settlement. There are no extant historic Mormon buildings at this site.

## Historical Background

Also known as Yelrome (Morley spelled backwards with an extra "e"), Morley's Settlement was founded in 1839 when Isaac Morley purchased a small cabin three miles northeast of Lima, Adams County.

Several prominent Mormon families lived in Yelrome, including those of Alpheus Cutler, Enos Curtis, Orville Cox, Edmond Durfee, Solomon Hancock, and Thomas Hickenlooper. On Sunday, 14 May 1843, the Saints at Morley's Settlement heard Joseph Smith preach. Wilford Woodruff recorded:

> Sunday — The meeting was opened by singing, and prayer by Wilford Woodruff. Then Joseph the Seer arose and said it is not wisdom that we should have all knowledge at once presented before us but that we should have a little then we can comprehend it. He then read the second Epistle of Peter 1*st* chapter, sixteen to last verse and dwelt upon the 19*th* verse with some remarks. Add to your faith knowledge etc. The principle of knowledge is the principle of salvation . . . The principle of salvation is given to us through the knowledge of Jesus Christ . . . Then knowledge through our Lord and savior Jesus Christ is the grand key that unlocks the glories and mysteries of the kingdom of heaven . . . Many other very useful remarks were made on the occasion by Joseph the Seer.[16]

The community had almost four hundred twenty-five members before it was abandoned. During the fall of 1845 outlying Mormon settlements became vulnerable to mob action. Both Lima and Morley's Settlement were attacked in September. On Thursday 11 September the Church in Nauvoo received the following letter from Yelrome, written by Solomon Hancock:

> Dear Brother, I will agreeably to your request send you some of the particulars of what has been done, on the other side of the branch, it is a scene of desolation. On Wednesday the 10th all of a sudden, the mob rushed upon Edmund Durfee and destroyed some property, and set fire to both of his buildings . . . On the morning of the 11th they again set fire to the buildings of Edmund Durfee, and fired upon some of his children without hitting them; they then proceeded to the old shop of Father Morley's and set fire to both his shops . . . In the afternoon the mob came on again and set fire to Father Whiting's chair shop, Walter Cox, Cheney Whiting and Azariah Tuttle's houses, at evening they retreated back again. . . . Last evening they set on fire three buildings, near Esq. Walker's; and this morning

we expect them to renew their work of destruction . . . the mob is determined to destroy us.[17]

A few weeks later, on 15 November, a mob shot and killed Edmund Durfee. The community lay in ashes and was abandoned by the Saints as they moved to the relative safety of Nauvoo.

# 5. Lima, Adams County, Illinois

Lima is on Highway 96 south of Nauvoo, Warsaw, and the turn-off to Morley's Settlement. Several Saints are buried in the Lima Cemetery. There are no extant historic buildings from the Mormon period.

## Historical Background

Lima was an important agricultural community during the Mormon period. A stake was organized in the fall of 1840. When mob violence broke out in Hancock County, it quickly spread to Adams County, and to Lee County, Iowa. A large anti-Mormon party was well established in Quincy by the summer of 1845. Because the settlement of Lima was between Quincy and Warsaw, the other site of anti-Mormon activity, Mormon leaders were concerned that crops would be destroyed. John Taylor reported:

> Thursday, September 11th, 1845. — This morning we received information from Lima, that the mobs were burning houses there; the first report was that there was one burnt; next report that came was, there were four burnt; and finally we heard that there were three burnt. We [the Twelve] held a council and thought it advisable as we were going west in the spring to keep all things as quiet as possible and not resent anything. After the trouble we had to finish the Temple to get our endowments, we thought it of more importance than to squabble with the mob about property, seeing that the houses were not much importance, and no lives were taken. Thinking by these specific measures that they would be likely not to molest us; and to show the surrounding country that we were orderly disposed people, and desirous of keeping peace. It was also counselled that the brethren from the surrounding settlements should come into Nauvoo with their grain.
>
> Friday, September 12th, 1845. — Reports came in about their further mobbing. We sent a number of teams off for grain to the settlements.[18]

Brigham Young explained the Church policy:

The object of our enemies [burning our settlements] is to get opposition enough to raise popular excitement but we think it best to let them burn up our homes while we take care of our families and grain. Let the sheriff of Hancock county attend to the mob, and let us see whether he and the Jack-Mormons, so called, the friends of law and order, will calmly sit down and watch the funeral procession of Illinois liberty."[19]

# 6. Quincy, Adams County, Illinois

Quincy is on Highway 96, approximately 43 miles south of Nauvoo. Highway 96 merges with Highway 24, in turn becoming North Third Street in Quincy. Continue on North Third Street (it runs north and south) to the intersection of Maine Street. Turn east (left) on Maine and proceed one block to Fourth Street.

**Washington Park** is on the block southeast of the intersection of North Fourth and Maine Streets, only 4 blocks from the Mississippi River. The park is the site of the main camping ground of the Saints who were driven from Missouri in 1839. A marker commemorating the Mormons' campground is located on the south side of the park.

### Historical Background
Members of the Mormon Church fled across the Mississippi River from Missouri to Illinois during the winter of 1838. The citizens of Quincy opened their homes and offered assistance to these destitute people with extraordinary compassion.

Even before the Saints came to Adams County, it was one of the largest population centers in the state, and Quincy, its county seat, was reputed to be one of the finer towns on the upper Mississippi. In spite of the warm welcome and prospects available to the Saints in Adams County, they looked for another site to build their city.

Many of them had crossed into Missouri earlier via Quincy to build their New Zion and prepare for the New Jerusalem. Now they returned to Quincy for protection from the persecution they found in the land of promise. The people of Quincy fed, clothed, and sheltered the Saints. Camps could be found up and down the river banks, with as many as sixteen hundred Saints camped near the City Park (Washington). Emma Smith and her children stayed at the Cleveland home, a few miles out of town. Within a short time the prophet himself arrived. Brigham Young, Wilford Woodruff, and other Church leaders soon visited him there. Woodruff recorded:

> May 3rd   This was an interesting day to my soul. I left Quincy in company with five others of the Twelve and rode four miles out of town to Mr. Cleveland's to visit Brother Joseph Smith Jr. and his family. We arrived at his house and once more had the happy privilege of taking Brother Joseph by the hand. Two years had rolled away since I had seen his face. He greeted us with great joy. He had just received deliverance from prison and the hand of his enemies and returned to the bosom of his family . . . Joseph was frank, open and familiar as usual. Sister Emma was truly happy. The bishops of the Church were present also and after spending the day rejoicing together we returned to Quincy.[20]

A few days later a Church conference in Quincy sanctioned the purchase of land in Hancock County and in Iowa.

Quincy–Washington Park. Photograph courtesy of Historical Society of Quincy.

# 7. Montrose, Lee County, Iowa

Montrose is across the Mississippi River from Nauvoo. Take Highway 96 north from Nauvoo to Highway 9 (the Fort Madison turn off). Go west on Highway 9 and cross the river to Fort Madison. Turn south (left) on Highway 61. Drive 12 miles south to the Montrose turn-off. This becomes First Street in Montrose.

**Fort Des Moines.** At the first stop sign on First Street, turn east (left) on Main Street, and cross the railroad tracks to River Front Park, the site of the abandoned Fort Des Moines, where many of the Saints found shelter in 1839. A plaque commemorates the building of the fort.

### Historical Background

Isaac Galland moved his family across the river from Commerce (Nauvoo) in 1829.[21] That same year the U.S. Government granted the Sac and Fox Indian tribes almost 200,000 acres of land, known as the Half-Breed Tract, which was surveyed and divided among all lawful claimants by an Equity Court in Iowa Territory. In 1834, Galland and other speculators began to buy up land in the area.

Montrose, Iowa. Photograph courtesy of Harold Allen.

Fort Des Moines had been established in 1834 by the War Department but was abandoned in 1837 as the area became increasingly settled by whites, and the dragoons were moved farther west. Soon a town site, called Montrose, was laid out south of the fort.

In 1839, several Mormon families, including those of Israel Barlow, John Taylor, Wilford Woodruff, and Brigham Young, took up temporary residence in the vacant barracks of the fort. They initiated talks with Galland about buying land and the barracks.

Shortly after their arrival from Missouri, many of the Saints were sick with malaria and weak from the physical exhaustion of the forced exodus. Almost every family suffered illness during this period. Joseph and Hyrum Smith, Brigham Young, and other elders of the Church administered (gave a priesthood blessing) to many of the sick. Wilford Woodruff then witnessed healings:

[July] 22    Joseph was in Montrose and it was a day of God's power. There were many sick among the Saints on both sides of the river and Joseph went through the midst of them taking them by the hand and in a loud voice commanding them in the name of Jesus Christ to arise from their beds and be made whole and they leaped from their beds made whole by the power of God. Elder Elijah Fordham was one among the number and he with the rest of the sick rose from his bed and followed Joseph from house to house and it was truly a time of rejoicing.[22]

Montrose, Iowa. Photograph courtesy of Harold Allen.

Joseph Smith continued the negotiations for land, bargaining with Galland for property on both sides of the river—in Adams County, Iowa, and Hancock County, Illinois. The land was purchased in 1839. There were about 20,000 acres in Iowa, including the town of Nashville, and parts of the towns of Keokuk and Montrose, both part of the Half-Breed Tract. The purchase of this property was made possible by issuing Half Breed Land Company stock. During the Mormon period, several communities in Iowa were settled or inhabited by Mormons. In 1841, Zarahemla had 326 members; Ambroisa, 109 members; Nashville, 90 members; Meaham Settlement, 65 members; Keokuk, 13 members; Augusta, 50 members; Van Buren Township, 11 members; and Chequest Township, 30 members. There is evidence that a few Saints also settled in Pleasant Grove, Timothy Block Settlement, and Hawley Settlement.

Mormons were settling on both sides of the river. Farms and orchards sprang up around the city as the community of Nauvoo expanded, moving beyond its original plat map. A Mormon presence was found in several communities in the environs of Nauvoo such as Lima, Quincy, and Ramus. These communities continued as important satellites to Nauvoo, even when Church leaders, concerned about building the temple and gathering the Saints, encouraged the settlers to draw close to Nauvoo.

Since the Mississippi River divided the two principal Mormon settlements in Illinois and Iowa, the Nauvoo High Council moved quickly to establish control of the ferryboat running between Montrose and Nauvoo, and controlled its operation until the exodus in 1846.

By the fall of 1846 the Saints had nearly evacuated Nauvoo. Many were camped along the trail leading to Winter Quarters, Nebraska, where Brigham Young had established a temporary Church headquarters. While many Saints made their way to Winter Quarters, a few hundred Mormons remained in Nauvoo, either too sick or too poor to move across the river. (Some of these were recent converts who had just arrived in Nauvoo and were now without funds to continue their trip west). In late August 1846, several vigilante groups stepped-up pressure on these Mormons. Finally, the anti-Mormons attacked them in what has become known as the Battle of Nauvoo, a week of skirmishes in which several Mormons were killed, including Captain William Anderson, his son Augustus, and David Norris.[23]

After four days of skirmishes, the defenders surrendered. These Saints were then forced to cross the river to Montrose, where they

Potter's Slough near Montrose; traditionally identified as the site of the miracle of the quail. Photograph courtesy of LDS Historical Department.

were critically short of supplies and shelter. As many as 700 refugees were camped along the banks of the Mississippi River. Many had neither wagon nor tent to protect themselves from the elements. Food was scarce. Many starved or died from exposure during the next few days.

When news of this situation reached Brigham Young, he sent supplies to relieve their suffering and to bring them to the main staging grounds at Winter Quarters. Twenty wagons, seventeen oxen, forty-one cows, and several volunteers arrived on 6 October.

On 9 October 1846, before starting their movement westward, these Saints witnessed what to them was a miracle from God. As the Lord fed the Children of Israel in the wilderness with manna, a flock of quail landed in the Saints' camp. The birds were exhausted and easy to kill. These birds provided much needed nourishment for the camp.[24]

A second rescue mission was sent from Winter Quarters, arriving in late October to assist those still remaining. By November 1846, those who wanted to go west had been evacuated to Winter Quarters, where they waited for spring to begin their journey to the Great Basin.

# 8. Sugar Creek, Lee County, Iowa

Sugar Creek is approximately six miles west of Montrose. Go west on Main Street (Highway 404) in Montrose to the junction with Highway 61. Continue west (left) on Highway 61 to the junction with Highway 218. Turn north and drive about one mile to J 72, a county road. Turn west (left) on J 72 and go about three miles to the concrete bridge crossing Sugar Creek. The 1846 Sugar Creek staging grounds was both north and south of this bridge. The campground was located on the northeast bank of the creek.

## Historical Background

Charles Shumway arrived early at the ferry dock in Nauvoo on the morning of 4 February 1846. He was the first in a long wave of refugee–emigrants awaiting the flat-bottomed ferry boats that would

Sugar Creek, Iowa. Photograph courtesy of the authors.

take the Saints' wagons, loaded with their possessions, across the Mississippi River to the Iowa side. In the next several days a large company of Saints made their way to Sugar Creek, some six miles to the southwest of Montrose.

After Joseph Smith's assassination, anti-Mormon activity had escalated, prompting an urgent effort during 1846 to remove the Saints from all settlements and encampments in Iowa and Illinois. As many as eight hundred Saints were located on the banks of Sugar Creek by the end of February. Many of them had less than two weeks worth of provisions.[25] Several accidents occurred during these first days. For example, Capt. Luddington "in getting his wagons away . . . got his hand mashed very badly," Hosea Stout recorded.[26]

These first weeks at Sugar Creek were even more difficult because of inclement weather and scant preparation. The Saints gathered in makeshift shelters on the Iowa side of the river waiting for spring before beginning their long journey west. Hosea Stout related his own situation:

> [I] prepared for the night by erecting a temporary tent out of bed clothes. At this time my wife was hardly able to set up and my little son was sick with a very high fever and would not even notice any thing that was going on.[27]

Lorenzo Snow recorded the difficulties in the camp:

> I left Nauvoo with part of my family on the 9th of February 1846. Camped at Sugar Creek where we remained until the first of March. This place is about nine miles from the city in the Territory of Iowa. After we arrived at Sugar Creek we sewed a couple of wagon covers together that were not in use and made them into a very comfortable tent; having got away in so much haste that we were not so well prepared. . . . So with two wagons and a tent we made ourselves as comfortable as the circumstances of the weather would admit. There were a hundred families gathered in there before us and others were now constantly arriving. We had been but few days in camp when we had to put up with the inconvenience of a heavy snow storm. The weather turned severely cold and the Mississippi froze so hard that teams and heavy laded wagons crossed over with perfect safety.[28]

# APPENDIX 1

## GLOSSARY OF ARCHITECTURAL TERMS

ARCHED ENTRANCE   Door opening with a semicircular top, often incorporating fan and oval forms. See photograph page 218t (top).

ARCHITRAVE   A beam resting on columns or on a wall; the lowest of the three parts of an entablature.

BALUSTRADE   A series of balusters (small posts) which support a rail, thus making an open fence for a stair, porch, terrace, etc. A solid fence in such places is called a PARAPET. 46, 47, 83, 220b, 222t

BARGEBOARD   A board, often ornately curved, attached to the projecting edges of a gabled roof. 165

CAPITAL   The decorated top part of a column or pilaster, crowning the shaft and supporting the entablature. It is a decorative transition from vertical support to horizontal burden. 98

CORNICE   A horizontal molding projecting along the top of a wall or building, often called a crown molding. When a cornice is part of an entablature, it is the highest of the three parts. A non-horizontal cornice which follows the sloping roofline of a pediment is called a RAKING CORNICE. 111, 145, 211, 216b

DORIC   The oldest and simplest order of ancient Greek architecture, characterized by simplicity of form, and especially by fluted, heavy columns with no bases, simple capitals, and a frieze of alternating triglyphs and metopes. (Other Greek orders are Ionic and Corinthian, but only Doric was used much in Nauvoo.)

EAVES   (usually plural) The projecting overhang at the lower edge of a roof, extending beyond the walls of a building for better drainage. When an eave and its supporting cornice are projected around the corner of a building which has a pediment, these short projections are called RETURNED EAVES. 51, 65, 70, 82, 111, 145, 215, 220t

ENTABLATURE   An ornamental transition from support to roof: a horizontal superstructure, supported by columns or walls, and supporting a roof or pediment, etc. An entablature has three parts: architrave, frieze, and cornice. 89, 113, 138, 212, 216b

FANLIGHT   A semicircular or fan-shaped window with radiating mullions (dividing bars), often set over a door or window. 111, 211, 216t, 218b

FRIEZE   A horizontal band, often decorated with sculpture, etc.; the middle of the three parts of a building's entablature. 217t

HIP ROOF   A roof with sloping ends as well as sides. A roof may be hipped at both ends or one only. 108, 128

KEYSTONE   The central, uppermost, wedge-shaped block in a masonry arch, often accented by scale and ornament. 108, 141

LANCET   A narrow, pointed arch or window. 36

LINTEL   A beam of any material used to span an opening. 116, 138, 141, 217t

OGEE ARCH   A pointed arch with an S-shaped curve on each side. 94

PARAPET GABLE   (also called FIRE GABLE) A masonry gable wall outside the roof ends, which are fitted into the inside of the sloping gable instead of resting upon it. 53, 58, 77, 80, 83, 138, 211, 216t

PEDIMENT   A (usually) low-pitched, triangular gable formed by the sloping rooflines at the ends of a ridge-roofed building; a similarly-shaped structure over a doorway, window, niche, etc. 55, 65, 111, 145

PIER   A heavy column, usually square, used to support with, as at the end of an arch: a reinforcing part built out from the surface of a wall.

PILASTER   A rectangular support or pier projecting partially from a wall and treated architecturally as a column, with a base, shaft, and capital.

SALTBOX   A house type shaped like a saltbox (originating in colonial New England) having two stories in front and one at the rear, and a gable roof with a much longer slope at the rear. 94, 144

SIDELIGHT   A window at the side of a door. 108, 219b

STEPPED GABLE   A parapet gable wall which rises in steps rather than in the continuous roofline slope. 114, 117, 125, 168, 179

TRANSOM   A small window above a door or window. 65, 104, 108, 219b

TRIGLYPH   In a Doric frieze, the regularly-recurring, rectangular block, having two vertical grooves (glyphs), with a chamfer (or half groove) at each side, thus leaving three vertical ridges. In a Doric frieze, the triglyphs alternate with metopes (the spaces between). 97b

# APPENDIX 2

## ARCHITECTURE IN NAUVOO

Nauvoo was still a town built primarily of wood when the Saints left the city in 1846. Many of the unoccupied frame buildings erected by the Saints in the 1840s had been torn down by 1918. By 1940 numerous brick dwellings, deserted and in serious disrepair, had been razed. As a result, much of early Nauvoo has been lost. The more substantial structures, most of which were built by the leading members of the community, survived while most of the log cabins and frame homes have long since disappeared.

Several one-story brick residences of only two or three rooms are still in existence in the main portion of the old city. Their simple, functional form probably represents the residential environment of the average settler in the 1840s. Most of the homes were modest and plain in design, as evidenced in the central part of the Brigham Young House and kindred structures.

While it is impossible to reconstruct old Nauvoo as it really was, the restoration process has created a memorial to those early pioneers and settlers, and prevented the further deterioration of historic Nauvoo structures.

The photographs in this book are some of the best sources for expanding our view of the city beyond what we see today. From the photographs and the few surviving structures it is possible to envision some of the architectural influences in the city at the time of the Mormon settlement.

Many buildings reflected a variation of design elements from the Colonial, Federal, and Greek Revival styles. Life on a changing frontier limited the Saints' resources, but the town had passed beyond the log-cabin stage.

The citizens of Nauvoo were not wealthy; moreover, they had embarked on their project during a statewide depression. They were, however, not lacking in energy or fine craftsmanship. Every able person worked, including Brigham Young as carpenter and glazier and Heber Kimball as blacksmith and potter. Those without money for material bartered for it. They erected hundreds of buildings: shops for skilled craftsmen; stores and houses constructed of lumber rafted from Wisconsin; and solid buildings made from brick and lime produced in their own kilns.

Nearly all Mormon buildings were practical, box-like structures with gable roofs and single or double brick chimneys built into the end walls. Coming from cool climates, the builders knew from experience that a house with a compact shape and an enclosed chimney would conserve valuable heat.[1]

Nauvoo homes sometimes reveal their owners' origins. Former New Englanders often built neat Federal houses, while most New Yorkers chose the Greek Revival style for their homes. Some of the brick houses — Brigham Young's, for example — had crow-step gables typical of old Dutch houses in New York, while others had more plain stepped gables like the Federalist buildings of Virginia.

The Federal, or Adamesque, style flowered in the early decades of the nation. Conceived by the Adams brothers in Scotland in 1776, it was a creative amalgam of earlier styles. European architecture was influenced greatly by it, as was architecture in the American colonies. Federal style buildings are found throughout the cities and towns of the eastern seaboard, particularly in New England.

Federal style houses were usually made of brick, were square or rectangular, two or three stories high, and topped with a gabled roof. Door and window openings were beautifully scaled and articulated, frequently incorporating fan and oval forms. Moldings were narrow, chaste, and delicate. In the Heber C. Kimball home, the Federal tradition in structural proportion and detailing is evident. The Wilford Woodruff home and the Joseph Smith Mansion House are also Federalist in their proportions. The Kimball home has a perfect Federal entrance, with a glazed fanlight and attenuated three-quarter columns framing the door. However, it is a simplified version without

Heber C. Kimball home drawing courtesy of Harold Allen.

side panels, and the fan is only as wide as the door. Another typical feature of the Federal influence is the double chimneys (Kimball and Woodruff homes). In the Kimball home as it may have originally appeared in the 1840s, the end wall is an attempt to screen the gabled roof.

Many of Nauvoo's public buildings and homes reflected the dominance of the Greek Revival style in American architecture in the 1840s. The United States, with its democratic ideals, was considered the spiritual successor of ancient Greece, a feeling evident not only in the architecture but also in the very names of newly established towns — Athens, Sparta, and Ithaca.

Architect Alexander Jackson Davis complained in 1842 that it was difficult for strangers in American towns "to distinguish between a church, a bank and a hall of justice." He might have included houses in his list as well, for by this time the Greek temple-front was common in buildings both public and private.[2]

The most easily identifiable features of a Greek-inspired building are columns and pilasters. Most Greek Revival frame homes were

Orson Hyde home drawing courtesy of Harold Allen.

painted white, as was probably the case with the Orson Hyde home, shown here in a perspective drawing of the building as it may have appeared in the 1840s.

The flat corner pilasters, with simplified doric column caps and minimized entablature at the front door and with pilasters reflecting the character of the corner pilasters in a reduced scale, is such an example. In this design, the builder always tried to use the proportions so carefully developed by the Greek architects. In the Greek Revival style, there was no attempt to disguise the gable roof; in the Federal style, gable roofs were often hidden.

Other features of the Greek Revival style are bold, simple moldings on the exterior, as shown in the drawing of the Printing Complex. Note the returned eaves and the small-paned windows equipped with shutters and crowned by a fine entablature. In the Printing Complex and in the Orson Hyde home, the Greek Revival elements are dominant; yet they are used in a restrained manner and without the exuberance found in the more settled and affluent section of the eastern seaboard.

Various Nauvoo structures exemplify particular Greek-Revival details, such as a doorway with transom and side lights (Mansion House, Masonic Hall, and Printing Complex), a fan gable ornament or win-

Printing Complex drawing courtesy of Harold Allen.

dow (South Wing of Early Hotel, Coolidge home, and Printing Complex), continuous entablature forming a pediment (Coolidge home), returned eaves (Hyde home), a pilaster-borne entablature (Hyde and Mansion houses).[3]

While Nauvoo architecture was probably representative in many ways of its time, it nevertheless had some components seldom used in the Western Illinois region. The following photographs illustrate some detailed examples of Nauvoo architecture and design.

Mansion House Rain Gutter Capital. Photograph courtesy of
LDS Museum of Church History and Art.

The above rain gutter capital is from Joseph Smith's Mansion House
and is now housed in the LDS Museum of Church History and Art in
Salt Lake City. The Seventies' Hall Museum in Nauvoo has two examples of pressed tin rain gutters from the Mormon period. The Stoddard
Tinsmith shop was quite busy filling the needs for such building materials. Pressed tin was also used as a roofing material in Nauvoo — a few
examples can be seen today in "upper" Nauvoo.

Some homes had features unusual for Nauvoo structures. In the
photographs below uncommon detailing is shown.

Cornerstone of Cultural Hall—M. Helm G.M.A.L. 5843 (M. Helm Grandmaster after light 5843, i.e. 1843). Photograph courtesy of Harold Allen.

Entablature and Pilaster Capital of the Orson Hyde home. Photograph courtesy of Harold Allen.

Doubled chimneys on the north wall of the Wilford Woodruff home. Photograph courtesy of Harold Allen.

West gable of John Smith home. Photograph courtesy of Harold Allen.

An unusual ornamented frieze. Photograph courtesy of Harold Allen.

Fan gable ornament on the Early Hotel. Photograph courtesy of Harold Allen.

Brick cornice on the Raymond Clark Store, similar to one on the Heber C. Kimball home. Photograph courtesy of Harold Allen.

Arched entrance of the Heber C. Kimball home. Photograph courtesy of Harold Allen.

Scroll-sawed treatment of the Bishop Hunter home.
Photograph courtesy of Harold Allen.

Greek Revival entrance of the Printing Complex.
Photograph courtesy of Harold Allen.

Returned eave of a frame home. Photograph courtesy of Harold Allen.

Inscription Stone on the Heber C. Kimball home.
Photograph courtesy of Harold Allen.

Door, painted to imitate burl, in the Printing Complex.
Photograph courtesy of Harold Allen.

Wooden fireplace, painted to simulate marble, in the Printing Complex.
Photograph courtesy of Harold Allen.

Newel in front hall of the Mansion House. Photograph courtesy of Harold Allen.

Greek Revival fireplace in the Mansion House.
Photograph courtesy of Harold Allen.

In Nauvoo, only the temple combined a distinctive architectural mass and original details reflecting the religion of the Latter-day Saints. Joseph Smith and the temple architect, William Weeks, did not regard the building as belonging outside the tradition of American architecture, for the temple certainly manifested contemporary trends. It represented, rather, an effort to compete with the architecture of the non-Mormon world on its own terms. The temple was a highly original building, its awkwardness due in part to the attempt to create an architectural identity for a new people with an uncommon religion.

The temple was built on a grand scale with pilasters on all four sides and a four-section tower crowning the mass. Religious symbols adorned the pilasters and the entablature. There were thirty moon, sun, and star stones used in the design.[4]

Drawing of the Nauvoo Temple, courtesy of Harold Allen.

Temple on the hill photograph.

# APPENDIX 3

## TEMPLE ON THE HILL PHOTOGRAPH

Probably the most famous photograph of Nauvoo is entitled the "temple on the hill" or the "outhouse."

This daguerreotype may have been taken by Lucian Foster in the early spring of 1846. It was probably taken from somewhere in the vicinity of Foster's Daguerrean Gallery near the corner of Parley and Hyde Streets. Several of the buildings in the photograph are still standing.

The following identification of the buildings in this photograph is based upon current research and an article in the *Church News* dated 6 November 1965, researched by Rowena Miller. The following numbers correspond with the numbers placed on the photograph: 1) Temple; 2) possibly the Parley P. Pratt home and store; 3) Amos Davis home and store; 4) Robert Foster Hotel; 5) Heber C. Kimball home; 6) Samuel Williams home; 7) William E. Horner, Abram Hoover, or John Wilkie home; 8) Albert Brown home; 9) Brick Stable; 10) Silas Condit home; 11) Lucian Woodworth home; 12) Noble-Smith yard; 13) Joseph W. Coolidge yard; 14) Parley Street.

# NOTES

**Preface**

1. Scott G. Kenney, ed., *Wilford Woodruff's Journal: 1833–1898, Typescript* (Midvale, Utah: Signature Books, 1983), 3:49.

**Introduction**

1. See William G. McLoughlin, *Revivals, Awakenings, and Reform: An Essay on Religion and Social Change in America, 1607–1977* (Chicago: University of Chicago Press, 1978). For a fuller treatment of this period of LDS Church history (1830–1838), see Leonard J. Arrington and Davis Bitton, *The Mormon Experience: A History of the Latter-day Saints* (New York: Alfred A. Knopf, 1979).

2. See Whitney R. Cross, *The Burned-over District* (Ithaca, New York: Cornell University Press, 1982).

3. For more information on the life of Joseph Smith during this period see Richard L. Bushman, *Joseph Smith and the Beginnings of Mormonism* (Urbana: University of Illinois Press, 1984).

4. For an RLDS church interpretation of these events, see Richard P. Howard, "Joseph Smith's First Vision: The RLDS Tradition," *Journal of Mormon History* 7 (1980): 23–30.

5. Prior to 26 April 1838, the Church was known as "The Church of Christ," "The Church of Jesus Christ," "The Church of God," and, by conference action, "The Church of the Latter Day Saints." The Church was nicknamed "Mormons" or "Mormonites" by their opponents. The name was officially changed to "The Church of Jesus Christ of Latter Day Saints" in April 1838. The LDS church in Utah today varies the capitalization slightly: "Latter-day Saints" instead of "Latter Day Saints."

6. For a history of the Mormons in Kirtland, see Milton V. Backman, Jr., *The Heavens Resound: A History of the Latter-day Saints in Ohio 1830–1838* (Salt Lake City, Utah: Deseret Book, 1983).

7. For a discussion of these events see Stephen C. LeSueur, *The 1838 Mormon War in Missouri* (Columbia, Missouri: University of Missouri Press, 1987). For an alternative view on certain aspects of the Missouri experience, see Dean C. Jessee and David J. Whittaker, eds., "The Last Months of Mormonism in Missouri: The Albert Perry Rockwood Journal," in *BYU Studies* 28 (Winter 1988): 5–41.

8. Parley P. Pratt, *Autobiography of Parley P. Pratt* (Salt Lake City, Utah: Deseret Book Company, 1968), 277–78.

9. Quoted in Donald Q. Cannon, in "Spokes on the Wheel: Early Latterday Settlements in Hancock County, Illinois," *The Ensign of the Church of Jesus Christ of Latter-day Saints* (February 1986): 62–68.

**Early Nauvoo and Nauvoo Today**

1. Scott H. Faulring, ed., *An American Prophet's Record: The Diaries and Journals of Joseph Smith* (Salt Lake City, Utah: Signature Books, 1987), 474.

2. See Donald L. Enders, "The Steamboat Maid of Iowa: Mormon Mistress of the Mississippi," *BYU Studies* 19 (Spring 1979): 321–35.

3. Autobiography of Mosiah Hancock, Special Collections, Harold B. Lee Library, Brigham Young University.

4. Faulring, 300.

5. Ibid., 335.

6. Quoted in James B. Allen, "To the Saints in England: Impressions of a Mormon Immigrant (The 10 December 1840 William Clayton letter from Nauvoo to Manchester)," *BYU Studies* 18 (Spring 1978), 475–80.

7. Faulring, 475.

8. See Lawrence G. Coates, "Brigham Young and Mormon Indian Policies: The Formative Period, 1836–1851," *BYU Studies* 18, (Spring 1978), 428–52.

9. Quoted in Kenneth W. Godfrey, Audrey M. Godfrey, and Jill Mulvay Derr, *Women's Voices: An Untold History of the Latter-day Saints, 1830–1890* (Salt Lake City, Utah: Deseret Book Company, 1982), 124–25.

10. Maureen Ursenbach, "Eliza R. Snow's Nauvoo Journal," *BYU Studies* 15 (Summer 1975), 404.

11. Dean C. Jessee, ed., *The Personal Writings of Joseph Smith* (Salt Lake City, Utah: Deseret Book, 1984), 482.

12. *Nauvoo Neighbor*, 14 August 1844.

13. See Dean C. Jessee, "The Reliability of Joseph Smith's History," *Journal of Mormon History* 3:23–46.

14. *Times and Seasons*, 2 August 1841.

15. Godfrey, Godfrey, and Derr, *Women's Voices*, 135–37.

16. Maureen Ursenbach Beecher, ed., "All Things Move in Order in the City: The Nauvoo Diary of Zina Diantha Huntington Jacobs," *BYU Studies* 19 (Spring 1979), 317.

17. Andrew F. Ehat and Lyndon W. Cook, eds., *The Words of Joseph Smith* (Provo, Utah: Brigham Young University Religious Studies Center, 1980), 106–7.

18. These quotations come from Thomas Bullock's and Wilford Woodruff's accounts, 7 April 1844. See Ehat and Cook, *The Words of Joseph Smith*, 343, 354.

19. For a discussion of the importance and the recording of this sermon, see Donald Q. Cannon, "The King Follett Discourse: Joseph Smith's Greatest Sermon in Historical Perspective," *BYU Studies* 18 (Winter 1978): 179–92; Stan Larson, "The King Follett Discourse: A Newly Amalgamated Text," *BYU Studies* 18 (Winter 1978): 209–25.

20. Two other major sites for meetings were the East Grove and the temple site itself. For contemporary accounts of these Nauvoo discourses, see Andrew F. Ehat and Lyndon W. Cook, eds., *The Words of Joseph Smith*.

21. See James B. Allen, "One Man's Nauvoo: William Clayton's Experience in Mormon Illinois," *Journal of Mormon History* 6 (1979): 37–60.

22. William Law Journal, 15 April 1844, in private possession.

23. Kenney, 2:382.

24. Andrew F. Ehat, "They Might Have Known That He Was Not 'a Fallen Prophet'—The Nauvoo Journal of Joseph Fielding," *BYU Studies* 19 (Winter 1979): 147–48.

25. See Nelson B. Wadsworth, *Through Camera Eyes* (Provo, Utah: Brigham Young University Press, 1975), 7–12.

26. Kenney 2:449–450.

27. Juanita Brooks, ed., *On the Mormon Frontier: The Diary of Hosea Stout, 1844–1861* (Salt Lake City, Utah: University of Utah Press, 1964) 1:27–28.

28. Willard Richards, *Willard Richards Journals* 26 March 1845.

29. *Hancock Eagle* 3 April 1846.

30. B.H. Roberts, *The Rise and Fall of Nauvoo* (Salt Lake City, Utah: The Deseret News, 1900), 19, 369.

31. Wadsworth, 165.

32. On 25 August 1919, several members of the RLDS Church visited Nauvoo. Their photographs and descriptions included block numbers and some research to verify their site identifications. It is one of the best accounts published of either LDS or RLDS material during this early period. See Herman C. Smith, "Travels," *Journal of History* 7 (January 1914): 5–21 and Mark H. Siegfried, "Description of Historic Places in Nauvoo," *Journal of History* 13 (January 1920): 1–8. Several LDS members reported their visits, including John Zimmerman Brown, "Nauvoo Today," *Improvement Era* 12: 468 ff. and Andrew Jenson, *Autobiography of Andrew Jenson* (Salt Lake City, Utah: Deseret News Press, 1938), 173–85.

33. For a discussion of American architectural styles, see John C. Poppeliers, S. Allen Chambers, Jr., and Nancy B. Schwartz, *What Style Is It? A*

*Guide to American Architecture* (Washington, D.C.: The Preservation Press, 1983).

34. Quoted by Stanley B. Kimball, "Nauvoo," *The Improvement Era* 65 (July 1962): 548.

**Guided Tours**

1. Architectural descriptions and information contained in Appendices 1 and 2 are based on Robert M. Lillibridge, "Architectural Currents on the Mississippi River: Nauvoo, Illinois," *Journal of the Society of Architectural Historians* 19 and 3 (1960): 109–114; Laurel B. Andrew, "Symbolism in Nauvoo," *Early Mormon Temples: The Architecture of the Millennial Kingdom in the West* (Albany, New York: State University New York Press, 1978); Betty I. Madden, "Nauvoo, the Utopia," *Art, Crafts, and Architecture in Early Illinois* (Urbana, Illinois: University of Illinois Press, 1974), 195–208; and James Langenheim, senior partner of Langenheim and Associates in La Crescenta, California.

2. Lisle G. Brown's "The Sacred Departments for Temple Work in Nauvoo: The Assembly Room and the Council Chamber," *BYU Studies* 19 (Spring 1979): 361–74.

3. Beecher, "Nauvoo Diary of Zina," 311.

4. Juanita Brooks, ed., *On the Mormon Frontier: The Diary of Hosea Stout, 1844–1861* (Salt Lake City, Utah: University of Utah Press, 1964) 1:64.

5. Heber C. Kimball, "Journal," *The Church of Jesus Christ of Latter-day Saints Church Archives* (LDSCA), Salt Lake City, Utah.

6. See Michael Quinn, "The Practice of Rebaptism at Nauvoo," *BYU Studies* 18 (Winter 1979), 226–32.

7. Juanita Brooks, *On the Mormon Frontier* 1:66.

8. The biographical material given relates to the individual identified by the modern designation of the site, such as the BRIGHAM YOUNG HOME; women and children who were occupants of the site are mentioned only briefly, if at all, in this section. The information has been gathered from various sources, some of which present conflicting information on dates, places, and spelling. The principal source materials of this information are Lyndon Cook, *The Revelations of the Prophet Joseph Smith* (Salt Lake City, Utah: Deseret Book Company, 1985); Susan Easton Black, *Membership of the Church of Jesus Christ of Latter-day Saints: 1830–1848* (Provo, Utah: Religious Studies Center Department of Church History and Doctrine, BYU, 1989); and information provided by Corey Merrick at the LDS Church Family History Library, Salt Lake City, Utah.

9. Amos Davis, "Ledger Account Book", LDSCA, Salt Lake City, Utah.

10. Harold Schindler, *Orrin Porter Rockwell: Man of God — Son of Thunder* (Salt Lake City: University of Utah Press, 1966), 80–81.

11. Faulring, 442.

12. See Lyndon W. Cook, "William Law, Nauvoo Dissenter," *BYU Studies* 14 (Winter 1982): 47–72.

13. Faulring, 489.

14. William Law, "Journal", in private possession. See also Wilson Law's deposition dated 22 August 1844 in Steven G. Barnett, "Wilson Law: A Sidelight on the *Expositor* Incident," *BYU Studies* 19 (Winter 1979): 245.

15. Quoted in Roger D. Launius, "Anti-Mormonism in Illinois: Thomas C. Sharp's Unfinished History of the Mormon War, 1845," *Journal of Mormon History* 15 (1989), 30.

16. For a discussion of the martyrdom see Davis Bitton, "The Martyrdom of Joseph Smith in Early Mormon Writings," *John Whitmer Historical Association Journal* 3 (1983): 29–39; Dean C. Jessee, "Return to Carthage: Writing the History of Joseph Smith's Martyrdom," *Journal of Mormon History* 8 (1981): 3–20; and Kenneth W. Godfrey, "Non-Mormon Views of the Martyrdom: A Look at Some Early Published Accounts," *John Whitmer Historical Association Journal* 7 (1987): 12–20.

17. *Wasp*, 29 October 1842.

18. David E. Miller, *Westward Migration of the Mormons* (Salt Lake City, Utah: n.p., 1963), 148–49.

19. Ehat and Cook, 381. For a discussion of the importance of this discourse see Richard L. Anderson "Joseph Smith's Final Self-Appraisal", *The Prophet Joseph Smith: Essays of the Lives and Missions of Joseph Smith*, edited by Larry C. Porter and Susan Easton Black (Salt Lake City: 1989), 320–32.

20. See Quinn, "Latter-day Prayer Circles," 79–105.

21. Quoted in Leonard J. Arrington, *Charles C. Rich* (Provo, Utah: Brigham Young University Press, 1974), 69.

22. Howard Coray, "Reminiscence" LDSCA, Salt Lake City, Utah.

23. Faulring, 244.

24. Drusilla Hendricks, "Reminiscence," LDSCA, Salt Lake City, Utah.

25. Stanley B. Kimball, *On the Potter's Wheel, The Diaries of Heber C. Kimball* (Salt Lake City, Utah: Signature Books, 1987), 104, 107, 109.

26. *Nauvoo Neighbor*, 24 January 1844.

27. For a full discussion of this aspect of Nauvoo history see Alvin E. Rust, *Mormon and Utah Coins and Currency* (Salt Lake City, Utah: Rust Rare Coins, Inc., 1984).

28. See James L. Kimball, Jr., "A Wall to Defend Zion: The Nauvoo Charter," *BYU Studies* 15 (Summer 1975): 491–97.

29. Kimball, *On the Potter's Wheel*, 130–31.

30. Joseph Smith, Jr., *History of The Church of Jesus Christ of Latter-day Saints*. Edited by B. H. Roberts (Salt Lake City, Utah: Deseret Book, 1951) 6:196–7.

31. Ehat and Cook, xii.

32. William Mulder and A. Russell Mortensen, eds., *Among the Mormons* (New York: Alfred A. Knopf, 1969), 118.

33. Ibid., 127–28.

34. Kate B. Carter, comp., "Bishop Edward Hunter," *Our Pioneer Heritage* (Salt Lake City, Utah: Daughters of Utah Pioneers, 1963), 318.

35. Kimball, *On the Potter's Wheel*, 110.

36. Ibid., 82.

37. J.D. Cummings, comp., "A brief sketch of the life of Mary Ann Yearsley," LDSCA, Salt Lake City, Utah.

38. Zora Smith Jarvis, *Ancestry Biography and Family of George A. Smith* (Provo, Utah: Brigham Young University Press, 1962), 102.

39. Brooks, *On the Mormon Frontier*, 1:22.

40. Ibid., 1:90.

41. For a summary of NRI's work see T. Edgar Lyon, "The Current Restoration in Nauvoo Illinois," *Dialogue* 5 (Spring 1970): 12–25.

42. *Nauvoo Neighbor*, 2 August 1843.

43. Lyon, "Recollections of 'Old Nauvooers'," 147–48.

44. Relief Society General Board, *History of Relief Society: 1842–1966* (Salt Lake City, Utah: The General Board of the Relief Society, 1966), 18.

45. For a discussion of the status of women see Anne Firor Scott, "Mormon Women, Other Women: Paradoxes and Challenges," *Journal of Mormon History* 13 (1986–87): 3–20.

46. Quoted in Linda King Newell, "Gifts of the Spirit," in *Sisters in Spirit*, edited by Maureen Ursenbach Beecher and Lavina Fielding (Urbana: University of Illinois Press, 1987), 115.

47. Jacob Weiler, "Reminiscences," LDSCA, Salt Lake City, Utah.

48. Willard Richards Journals, LDSCA, Salt Lake City, Utah. Willard Richards placed a gray stone on the vault and another under the coffin. Both stones were inscribed, "Jennetta Richards, born at Walkerfold, England, August 21, 1817. Married to Willard Richards September 24, 1838, died July 8, 1845." In 1958 the present memorial marker was placed by the Richards family of Salt Lake City on the grave, which had been moved in 1868.

49. Kenney, 2:233.

50. Kenney, 3:49, ff.

51. Quoted in T. Earl Pardoe's *Lorin Farr, Pioneer* (Provo, Utah: Brigham Young University Press, 1953), 70–72.

52. Kimball, *On the Potter's Wheel*, 128.

53. Erastus Snow Journal quoted in Andrew Karl Larson, *Erastus Snow: The Life of a Missionary and Pioneer for the Early Mormon Church* (Salt Lake City: The University of Utah Press, 1971), 97.

54. *Nauvoo Neighbor*, 5 June 1844.

55. Smith, *History of the Church*, 5:145.

56. Jarvis, 28.

57. The symbol of the sun with trumpets is common in New England cemetery headstones and often symbolizes the Day of Judgment. See Andrew, *Early Temples of the Mormons*, 82.

58. Perrigrine Sessions, "Journal", 30 January 1846, LDSCA, Salt Lake City, Utah.

59. See Smith's discourse on 27 August 1843 in Ehat and Cook, 243–245.

60. Josiah Quincy, *Figures of the Past* (Boston: Little, Brown, and Co., 1926), 386.

61. Eugene England, ed., "George Laub's Nauvoo Journal," *BYU Studies* 18 (Winter 1978): 171.

62. Ellis Sanders, "Papers," LDSCA, Salt Lake City, Utah.

63. William Mendenhall, "Nauvoo Journal, 2 May 1842–31 March 1847" LDSCA, Salt Lake City, Utah.

64. *Nauvoo Neighbor*, 30 October 1844.

65. *Nauvoo Neighbor*, 10 January 1844.

66. *Nauvoo Neighbor*, 12 July 1843.

67. *Nauvoo Neighbor*, 17 April 1844.

68. Quoted in Larsen, *Erastus Snow*, 102.

69. Della A. Belnap, "Collection," LDSCA, Salt Lake City, Utah.

70. Dean C. Jesse, "The John Taylor Nauvoo Journal January 1845–September 1845," *BYU Studies* 23 (Summer 1983): 47–48.

71. Vida E. Smith, "Two Widows of the Brick Row," *Journal of History* 3, (April 1910): 202–04.

72. Vinson Knight, "Letters," LDSCA, Salt Lake City, Utah.

73. George Riser, "Journal," at the University of Utah, Salt Lake City, Utah.

74. Kenney, 2:434.

75. Brigham Young, *Manuscript History of Brigham Young 1801–1844* (Salt Lake City, Utah: Elden J. Watson, 1971), 109, 130.

76. Quoted in Eugene England, *Brother Brigham*, (Salt Lake City, Utah: Bookcraft Inc., 1980), 77.

77. *Nauvoo Neighbor*, 6 September 1843.

78. Jessee, "The John Taylor Nauvoo Journal," 7.

79. Brigham Young, *Manuscript History of Brigham Young 1846–47* (Salt Lake City, Utah: Elden J. Watson, 1971), 30.

80. Ida Blum, *Nauvoo: Gateway to the West* (Carthage, Illinois: Journal Printing Company, 1978), 3.

81. *Times and Seasons*, 2 August 1841.

82. Louisa Tanner Follett, "1844–1845 September Diary," LDSCA, Salt Lake City, Utah.

83. Brown, "Nauvoo Today," 469.

84. Faulring, 246–48.

85. James Blakeslee, "Recollections and Diary": RLDS Auditorium Library, Independence, Missouri. Joseph Smith's history states, "There was a meeting at General William and Wilson Law's near the was mill . . . Several affidavits were taken and read against Joseph and others. William Law, Wilson

Law, Austin D. Cowles, John Scott Senior, Francis M. Higbee, Robert D. Foster, and Robert Pierce were appointed a committee to visit the different families of the city and see who would join the new church i.e., it was decided that Joseph was a fallen prophet and William Law was appointed in his place. Austin Cowles and Wilson Law Councilors. Robert D. Foster and Francis M. Higbee to the Twelve Apostles etc., as report says." Smith, *History of the Church*, 4:475.

86. William Law Journal, 1 January 1844. Someone crossed out the phrase beginning with "supper, we conversed" through "they were strongly disapproved."

87. Quoted in Andrew Jenson, "Joseph Smith, the Prophet," *The Historical Record* 7 (January 1888): 558.

88. For a discussion of this site see Robert T. Bray, *Times and Seasons: An Archaeological Perspective on Early Latter Day Saints Printing* (Colombia, Missouri: University of Missouri–Colombia, 1976).

89. Ebenezer Robinson, "Items of Personal History of the Editor," *The Return*, May–July 1890, 124.

90. Joseph Smith, *Teachings of the Prophet Joseph Smith*, comp. Joseph Fielding Smith (Salt Lake City, Utah: Deseret Book, 1976), 194.

91. Faulring, 292.

92. Ibid., 244.

93. Ibid., 224–45.

94. Ehat and Cook, 116–18.

95. LDS D&C 124:28, 41–42; and RLDS D&C 107:10d, 13b–c.

96. On special prayer circles see D. Michael Quinn, "Latter-day Prayer Circles," *BYU Studies* 19 (Fall 1978) :79–105. See also Lisle G. Brown, "The Sacred Departments for Temple Work in Nauvoo: The Assembly Room and the Council Chamber," *BYU Studies* 19 (Spring 1979): 361–74. On the law of adoption see Gordon Irving, "The Law of Adoption: One Phase of the Development of the Mormon Concept of Salvation, 1830–1900," *BYU Studies* 14 (Spring 1974): 291–314.

97. Roger Launius, a leading RLDS Church historian, notes that the RLDS church was a movement of dissenters. Its early members were Mormons who chose not to follow the main body of Saints west. Launius states that Jason Briggs was, in effect, the founder and first head of the Reorganization even though he was never its president/prophet.

98. For an excellent discussion of RLDS Church restoration goals at Nauvoo, see F. Mark McKiernan, *A Master Plan of the Historic Properties of the RLDS Church: Preserving and Interpreting Our Physical Heritage*.

99. Smith, *History of the Church*, 6:33.

100. Ibid., 4:437–438.

101. George Q. Cannon, *Life of Joseph Smith the Prophet* (Salt Lake City Utah: Deseret Book Company, 1958), 402.

102. Jessee, "The John Taylor Nauvoo Journal," 84–85.

103. Quoted in Dean C. Jessee, "The Original Book of Mormon Manuscript," *BYU Studies* 10 (Spring 1970): 264.

104. Quoted in ibid., 265.

105. James B. Allen and Thomas G. Alexander, eds., *Manchester Mormons: The Journal of William Clayton, 1840–1842* (Santa Barbara: Peregrine Smith, Inc., 1974), 200–201.

106. Quoted in Conway B. Sonne, *Saints on the Seas: A Maritime History of Mormon Migration, 1830–1890* (Salt Lake City, Utah: University of Utah Press, 1983), 96.

107. Faulring, 397.

108. Ibid., 471.

109. Kimball, *On the Potter's Wheel*, 85.

110. Lyon, "Recollections of 'Old Nauvooers'," 148.

111. Richard P. Howard, ed., *The Memoirs of President Joseph Smith III (1832–1914)* (Independence, Missouri: Herald Publishing House, 1979), 5, 19–20. During the reconstruction of the cabin at the Homestead this hiding place was located. Alma Blair kindly showed the authors the site in 1989.

112. For a detailed discussion of the city plat see Donald L. Enders, "Platting the City Beautiful: A Historical and Archeological Glimpse of Nauvoo Streets," *BYU Studies* 19 (Spring 1979): 408–15.

113. Quoted in Kimball, *Nauvoo*, 588.

114. Faulring, 416.

115. Ibid., 416–17.

116. Beecher, "Nauvoo Diary of Zina," 293.

117. Ronald K. Esplin, "Life in Nauvoo, June 1844: Vilate Kimball's Martyrdom Letters," *BYU Studies* 19 (Winter 1979): 238.

118. *Wasp*, 16 April 1842.

119. Mulder and Mortensen, 119–20.

120. Lyon, "Recollections," 145.

121. Faulring, 307.

122. Ivy H.B. Hill, *John Ensign Hill Diaries and Biographical Material* (Logan, Utah: S.P. Smith and Sons, 1962), 202–204.

123. Theodore Turley, "Reminiscences and Journal, 1839–1840 July," LDSCA, Salt Lake City, Utah.

124. For a partial list of those buried in Nauvoo see James C. Taylor and Donna Taylor, *Nauvoo Death and Burials: Old Nauvoo Burial Ground* (Nauvoo: Illinois: Nauvoo Restoration Inc., 1989); see also Susan Easton, *Inscriptions Found on Tombstones and Monuments in Early Latter-Day Saint Burial Grounds* (n.p., n.d).

125. *Wasp*, 4 June 1842.

126. Story found in Nauvoo file of William G. Hartley, Smith Institute for Church History, Brigham Young University.

127. B.H. Roberts, *A Comprehensive History of the Church of Jesus Christ of Latter-day Saints* 6 vols. (Salt Lake City, Utah: Deseret News Press, 1930) 2: 250.

128. Ibid., 248.

## Surrounding Communities

1. *Illinois State Register*, 20 March 1840.

2. See Davis Bitton, "American Philanthropy and Mormon Refugees, 1846–1849," *Journal of Mormon History* 7 (1980): 63–82.

3. "Agreement to Leave Nauvoo," in "Nauvoo City Collection," LDSCA, Salt Lake City, Utah.

4. "Nauvoo High Council Circular," 20 January 1846, LDSCA, Salt Lake City, Utah.

5. Willard Richards, "Willard Richards Journal," LDSCA, Salt Lake City, Utah.

6. Quoted in Dallin H. Oaks and Marvin S. Hill, *Carthage Conspiracy* (Urbana, Illinois: University of Illinois Press, 1975), 21.

7. B. H. Roberts, *The Life of John Taylor* (Salt Lake City, Utah: Bookcraft, Inc.), 144.

8. Oaks and Hill, 185.

9. Smith, *History of the Church*, 7: 420.

10. Quoted in Paul D. Ellsworth, "Mobocracy and the Rule of Law: American Press Reaction to the Murder of Joseph Smith," *BYU Studies* 20 (Fall 1979): 71–82.

11. For a discussion of these extracts see Bruce A. Van Orden, "Items of Instruction: Section 130 and 131," in *Harken O Ye People* (Sandy, Utah: Randall Book Company, 1984), 31–47.

12. Faulring, 340.

13. Quoted in Oaks and Hill, 126.

14. *Warsaw Signal*, 10 July 1844.

15. *Warsaw Signal*, 14 May 1845.

16. Kenney, 2:200–202.

17. Quoted in Jessee, "John Taylor Nauvoo Journal," 89–90.

18. Ibid., 88–89.

19. Ibid., 88.

20. Kenney, 1:329–30.

21. For a study of Galland see Lyndon W. Cook, "Isaac Galland—Mormon Benefactor," *BYU Studies* 19:3 (Spring 1979): 261–84.

22. Kenney, 1:347–48.

23. See Richard E. Bennett, "Eastward to Eden: The Nauvoo Rescue Missions," *Dialogue* 19 (Winter 1986): 100–108.

24. Russell Rich, *Ensign to the Nations: History of the LDS Church From 1846–1972* (Provo, Utah: Brigham Young University Press, 1973), 46.

25. For a discussion of this period see Susan W. Easton's "Suffering and Death on the Plains of Iowa," *BYU Studies* 21 (Fall 1981): 431–39.

26. Brooks, 1:124.

27. Ibid., 1:128.

28. Maureen Ursenbach Beecher, "The Iowa Journal of Lorenzo Snow," *BYU Studies* 24 (Summer 1984): 261–73.

**Appendix 2**

1. See Betty I. Madden, *Art, Crafts, and Architecture in Early Illinois* (Urbana, Illinois: University of Illinois Press, 1978), especially Chapter 16, "Nauvoo the Utopia," 196–28.

2. Quoted in C. Poppeliers, *What Style is it? A Guide to American Architecture* (Baltimore, Md.: National Trust for Historic Preservation in the United States), 36.

3. See Robert M. Lillibridge, "Architectural Currents on the Mississippi River Frontier: Nauvoo, Illinois," *Journal of the Society of Architectural Historians* 19 (October 1960): 109–14.

4. For a discussion of the Nauvoo Temple see Laurel B. Andrew, *The Early Temples of the Mormons: The Architecture of the Millennial Kingdom in the American West* (Albany, New York: State University of New York Press, 1978), especially Chapter 4, "Ritual and Symbolism at Nauvoo," 55–96.

# SELECTED BIBLIOGRAPHY
# OF PUBLISHED MATERIAL

## HISTORIES

**United States**

Billington, Ray Allen. *America's Frontier Heritage*. New York: Holt, Rinehart, and Winston, 1966.

Bushman, Richard L. "Family Security in the Transition from Farm to City, 1750–1850." In *The Underside of American History*, vol.1, edited by Thomas R. Frazier, 315–32. New York: Harcourt Brace Jovanovich, Publishers, 1987.

Russo, David J. *Families and Communities: A New View of American History*. Nashville, Tennessee: The American Association for State and Local History, 1974.

Smith, Page. *As a City upon a Hill: The Town in American History*. New York: Alfred A. Knopf, 1966.


**Illinois**

Angle, Paul M., ed. *Prairie State: Impressions of Illinois, 1673–1967, by Travelers and Other Observers*. Chicago: The University of Chicago Press, 1968.

Bateman, Newton, ed. *Historical Encyclopedia of Illinois* 2 vols. Chicago: Munsell Publishing Company, 1912.

Billington, Ray Allen. "The Frontier in Illinois History." *Journal of Illinois State Historical Society* 43 (1950): 28–45.

Calvin, Theodore. *The Frontier State, 1818–1848*. Chicago: Illinois Centennial Commission, 1918.

Doyle, Don H. *The Social Order of a Frontier Community: Jacksonville, Illinois, 1825–1870*. Urbana: University of Illinois Press, 1983.

Ford, Thomas. *A History of Illinois from Its Commencement as a State in 1818 to 1847*. Chicago: S.C. Greggs & Co., 1854.

Gregg, Thomas. *History of Hancock County, Illinois*. Chicago: Charles C. Chapman & Co., 1880.

Hancock County Board Of Supervisors. *History of Hancock County Illinois*. Carthage, Illinois: Journal Printing Company, 1968.

Lewis, Henry. *The Valley of the Mississippi Illustrated*. St. Paul: Minnesota Historical Society, 1967.

### Religion in America

Ahlstrom, Sydney E. *A Religious History of the American People*. New Haven, Conn.: Yale University Press, 1972.

Backman, Milton V., Jr. *Christian Churches of America: Origins and Beliefs*. New York: Charles Scribner's Sons, 1983.

Cross, Whitney R. *The Burned-over District*. Ithaca, New York: Cornell University Press, 1982.

Gaustad, Edwin Scott. *Dissent in American Religion*. Chicago: University of Chicago Press, 1973.

————, ed. *A Documentary History of Religion in America to the Civil War*. Grand Rapids, Mich.: William B. Eerdmans Publishing Company, 1982.

McLoughlin, William G. *Revivals, Awakenings, and Reform: An Essay on Religion and Social Change in America, 1607–1977*. Chicago: The University of Chicago Press, 1978.

### LDS/RLDS Church

Allen, James B., and Glen M. Leonard. *The Story of the Latter-day Saints*. Salt Lake City, Utah: Deseret Book, 1976.

Arrington, Leonard J., and Davis Bitton. *The Mormon Experience: A History of the Latter-day Saints*. New York: Alfred A. Knopf, 1979.

Barrett, Ivan J. *Joseph Smith and the Restoration: A History of the LDS Church to 1846*. Provo, Utah: Brigham Young University Press, 1973.

Berrett, William E. *The Latter-day Saints: A Contemporary History of the Church of Jesus Christ*. Salt Lake City, Utah: Deseret Book, 1985.

Blair, Alma R. "Reorganized Search of Jesus Christ of Latter Day Saints: Moderate Mormonism." In *The Restoration Movement: Essays in Mormon History*, edited by F. Mark McKiernan, Alma R. Blair and Paul M. Edwards, 207–30. Lawrence, Kansas: Coronado Press, 1973.

Hansen, Klaus J. *Mormonism and the American Experience*. Chicago: The University of Chicago Press, 1981.

Hill, Marvin S. *Quest For Refuge: The Mormon Flight from American Pluralism*. Salt Lake City, Utah: Signature Books, 1989.

————, and James B. Allen, eds. *Mormonism and American Culture*. New York: Harper & Row, Publishers, 1972.

Howard, Richard P. "Joseph Smith's First Vision: The RLDS Tradition." *Journal of Mormon History* 7 (1980): 23–30.

Launius, Roger D. "A New Historiographical Frontier: The Reorganized Church in the Twentieth Century." *John Whitmer Historical Association Journal* 6 (1986): 53–63.

Relief Society General Board. *History of Relief Society: 1842–1966*. Salt Lake City: The General Board of the Relief Society of the LDS Church, 1966.

Roberts, B.H. *A Comprehensive History of The Church of Jesus Christ of Latter-day Saints*, 6 vols. Salt Lake City, Utah: Deseret News Press, 1930.

Smith, Joseph Jr. *History of the Church of Jesus Christ of Latter-day Saints*. Edited by B.H. Roberts. 7 vols. Salt Lake City, Utah: Deseret Book, 1951.

Smith, Joseph III and Smith, Heman C., eds. *History of the Reorganized Church of Jesus Christ of Latter Day Saints*. 6 vols. Independence, Mo.: Herald Publishing House, 1973.

# IOWA AND NAUVOO

Bennett, Richard E. "Eastward to Eden: The Nauvoo Rescue Missions." *Dialogue* 19 (Winter 1986): 100–108.

Bitton, Davis. "American Philanthropy and Mormon Refugees, 1846–1849." *Journal of Mormon History* 7 (1980): 63–82.

Durham, Reed C., Jr. "The Iowa Experience: A Blessing in Disguise." *BYU Studies* 21 (Fall 1981): 463–74.

Easton, Susan W. "Suffering and Death on the Plains of Iowa." *BYU Studies* 21 (Fall 1981): 431–39.

Kimball, Stanley B. *Historic Sites and Markers Along the Mormon and Other Great Western Trails*. Urbana and Chicago: University of Illinois Press, 1988.

_____. "Nauvoo West: The Mormons of the Iowa Shore." *BYU Studies* 18 (Winter 1978): 132–42.

_____. "The Mormon Trail Network in Iowa 1838–1863: A New Look." *BYU Studies* 21 (Fall 1981): 417–30.

Pearson, Carol Lynn. " 'Nine Children Were Born': A Historical Problem from the Sugar Creek Episode." *BYU Studies* 21 (Fall 1981): 441–44.

Styles, Edward H. *Recollections and Sketches: Early Lawyers and Public Men of Iowa*. Des Moines, Iowa: Homestead Publishing Co., 1912.

Van Der Zee, Jacob. "The Half-Breed Tract." *Iowa Journal of History and Politics* 13 (1915): 151–64.

# NAUVOO

**General**

Blum, Ida. *Nauvoo: Gateway to the West*. Carthage, Illinois: Journal Printing Company, 1978.

Bushman, Richard L. "The Historian and Mormon Nauvoo." *Dialogue* 5 (Spring 1970): 51–61.

Cannon, Donald Q. "The Founding of Nauvoo." In *The Prophet Joseph: Essays on the Life and Mission of Joseph Smith*, edited by Larry C. Porter and Susan Easton Black, 246–60. Salt Lake City: Deseret Book Company, 1988.

Flanders, Robert Bruce. *Nauvoo: Kingdom on the Mississippi*. Urbana, Illinois: University of Illinois Press, 1965.

————. "Dream and Nightmare: Nauvoo Revisited." In *The Restoration Movement: Essays in Mormon History*, edited by F. Mark McKiernan, Alma R. Blair and Paul M. Edwards, 141–66. Lawrence, Kansas: Coronado Press, 1973.

Hampshire, Annette P. *Mormonism in Conflict: The Nauvoo Years*. New York: The Edwin Mellen Press, 1985.

Hansen, Klaus J. *Mormonism and the American Experience*. Chicago: University of Chicago Press, 1981.

Kimball, Stanley B. "Nauvoo." *The Improvement Era* 65 (July 1962): 512–17, 548–51.

————. "Nauvoo As Seen by Artists and Travelers." *The Improvement Era* 69 (January 1966): 38–43.

————. "The Mormons in Illinois, 1838–1848: A Special Introduction." *Journal of Illinois State Historical Society* 64 (Spring 1971): 4–21.

Leonard, Glen. "Recent Writing on Mormon Nauvoo." *Illinois Western Regional Quarterly* 11 (Fall 1988): 69–93.

————, and T. Edgar Lyon. "The Nauvoo Years." *Ensign* 9 (September 1979): 10–15.

McGavin, E. Cecil. *Nauvoo the Beautiful*. Salt Lake City, Utah: Bookcraft, Inc., 1972.

Miller, David E. *Westward Migration of the Mormons*. Salt Lake City: Utah: n.p., 1963.

————, and Della S. Miller. *Nauvoo: City of Joseph*. Santa Barbara: Peregrine Smith, Inc., 1974.

Poll, Richard D. "Nauvoo and the New Mormon History: A Bibliographical Survey." *Journal of Mormon History* 5 (1978): 105–23.

Roberts, B.H. *The Rise and Fall of Nauvoo*. Salt Lake City, Utah: Bookcraft, 1965.

Sanford, Mabel A. *Joseph's City Beautiful*. Independence, Mo.: Herald Publishing House, 1976.

Vance, Mary A. *Nauvoo, Illinois: A Bibliography*. Monticello, Illinois: Vance Bibliographies, 1980.

**Architecture**

Andrew, Laurel B. *The Early Temples of the Mormons: The Architecture of the Millennial Kingdom in the American West*. Albany: State University of New York Press, 1978.

Arrington, Joseph Earl. "Panorama Paintings in the 1840s of the Mormon Temple in Nauvoo." *BYU Studies* 22 (Spring 1982): 193–211.

Hayden, Dolores. *Seven American Utopias: The Architecture of Communitarian Socialism, 1790–1975.* Cambridge: MIT Press, 1976.

Lillibridge, Robert M. "Architectural Currents on the Mississippi River Frontier: Nauvoo, Illinois." *Journal of the Society of Architectural Historians* 19 (October 1960): 109–14.

Poppeliers, John C., S. Allen Chambers, Jr., and Nancy B. Schwartz. *What Style is it? A Guide to American Architecture.* Washington, D.C.: The Preservation Press, 1983.

### Biographical Studies

Allen, James B. *Trials of Discipleship: The Story of William Clayton, a Mormon.* Urbana, Illinois: University of Illinois Press, 1987.

_____."One Man's Nauvoo: William Clayton's Experience in Mormon Illinois." *Journal of Mormon History* 6 (1979): 37–60.

Anderson, Lavina Fielding. "They Came to Nauvoo." *Ensign* 9 (September 1979): 20–25.

_____."Joseph Smith's Brothers: Nauvoo and Afterwards." *Ensign* 9 (September 1979): 30–33.

Anderson, Richard Lloyd. "Joseph Smith's Final Self-Appraisal." In *The Prophet Joseph: Essays on the Life and Mission of Joseph Smith*, edited by Larry C. Porter and Susan Easton Black, 320–32. Salt Lake City, Utah: Deseret Book Company, 1989.

Arrington, J. Earl. "William Weeks, Architect of the Nauvoo Temple." *BYU Studies* 19 (Spring 1979): 337–59.

Arrington, Leonard J. *Charles C. Rich.* Provo, Utah: Brigham Young University Press, 1974.

_____. *Brigham Young: American Moses.* New York: Alfred A. Knopf, 1985.

Avery, Valeen Tippetts. "Sketches of the Sweet Singer: David Hyrum Smith, 1844–1904." *John Whitmer Historical Association Journal* 5 (1985): 3–15.

Avery, Valeen Tippetts, and Linda K. Newell. "Lewis C. Bidamon, Step Child of Mormondom." *BYU Studies* 22 (Winter 1980): 81–97.

Barnett, Steven G. "Wilson Law: A Sidelight on the *Expositor* Incident." *BYU Studies* 19 (Winter 1979): 245.

Barron, Howard H. *Orson Hyde: Missionary, Apostle, Colonizer.* Salt Lake City, Utah: Horizon Publishers, 1977.

Beecher, Maureen Ursenbach. "Leonora, Eliza, and Lorenzo: An Affectionate Portrait of the Snow Family." *Ensign* 10 (June 1980): 64–69.

Black, Susan Easton, comp. *Membership of the Church of Jesus Christ of Latter-day Saints: 1830–1848.* Provo, Utah: BYU Religious Studies Center, 1989. Fifty volumes.

Brooks, Juanita. *John D. Lee: Zealot, Pioneer Builder, Scapegoat.* Glendale, CA: The Arthur H. Clark Company, 1973.

Bushman, Richard L. *Joseph Smith and the Beginnings of Mormonism.* Urbana: University of Illinois Press, 1984.

Cannon, Donald Q., and David J. Whittaker, eds. *Supporting Saints: Life Stories of Nineteenth-Century Mormons.* Provo, Utah: BYU Religious Studies Center, 1985.

Cannon, George Q. *Life of Joseph Smith the Prophet.* Salt Lake City Utah: Deseret Book Company, 1958.

Carter, Kate B., comp. "Bishop Edward Hunter." In *Our Pioneer Heritage.* Salt Lake City, Utah: Daughters of Utah Pioneers, 1963.

Cook, Lyndon W. "Isaac Galland—Mormon Benefactor." *BYU Studies* 19 (Spring 1979): 261–284.

———. *Joseph Kingsbury: A Biography.* Provo, Utah: Grandin Books, 1985.

———. "William Law, Nauvoo Dissenter." *BYU Studies* 22 (Winter 1982): 47–72.

Corbett, Pearson H. *Hyrum Smith, Patriarch.* Salt Lake City, Utah: Deseret Book Company, 1971.

Cowley, Matthias F. *Wilford Woodruff: History of his Life and Labors.* Salt Lake City, Utah: Bookcraft, Inc., 1964.

Derr, Jill Mulvay. "Sarah Melissa Granger Kimball: The Liberal Shall Be Blessed." In *Sister Saints,* edited by Vicky Burgess/Olsen. Provo, Utah: Brigham Young University Press, 1978.

England, Breck. *The Life and Thought of Orson Pratt.* Salt Lake City, Utah: University of Utah Press, 1985.

England, Eugene. *Brother Brigham.* Salt Lake City, Utah: Bookcraft, Inc., 1980.

Esplin, Ronald K. "Inside Brigham Young: Abrahamic Tests as Preparation for Leadership." *BYU Studies* 20 (Spring 1980): 300–310.

———. "God Will Protect Me Until My Work Is Done." In *The Prophet Joseph: Essays on the Life and Mission of Joseph Smith,* edited by Larry C. Porter and Susan Easton Black, 280–319. Salt Lake City: Deseret Book Company, 1988.

Gregory, Thomas J. "Sidney Rigdon: Post Nauvoo." *BYU Studies* 21 (Winter 1981): 51–67.

Hartley, William G. *"They are my Friends," A History of the Joseph Knight Family, 1825–1850.* Provo, Utah: Grandin Book Company, 1986.

Hill, Donna. *Joseph Smith: The First Mormon.* Garden City, New York: Doubleday & Company, Inc., 1977.

Hill, Ivy H.B. *John Ensign Hill Diaries and Biographical Material.* Logan, Utah: S.P. Smith and Sons, 1962.

Hill, Marvin S. "Joseph Smith the Man: Some Reflections on a Subject of Controversy." *BYU Studies* 21 (Spring 1981): 175–86.

Hinckley, Brant S. *Daniel H. Wells*. Salt Lake City, Utah: Deseret News Press, 1942.

Howard, Richard P., ed., *The Memoirs of President Joseph Smith III (1832–1914)*. Independence, Missouri: Herald Publishing House, 1979.

Jarvis, Zora Smith. *Ancestry Biography and Family of George A. Smith*. Provo, Utah: Brigham Young University Press, 1962.

Jensen, Andrew. *Latter-day Saint Biographical Encyclopedia: A Compilation of Biographical Sketches of Prominent Men and Women in the Church*. 4 vols. Salt Lake City, Utah: Andrew Jensen History Co., 1901–1936.

Johnson, Benjamin F. *My Life's Review*. Independence, Missouri: Zion's Printing and Publishing Co., 1947.

Kimball, Stanley B. *Heber C. Kimball: Mormon Patriarch and Pioneer*. Urbana: University of Illinois Press, 1981.

Larson, Andrew Karl. *Erastus Snow: The Life of a Missionary and Pioneer for the Early Mormon Church*. Salt Lake City, Utah: The University of Utah Press, 1971.

Launius, Roger D. "William Marks and the Restoration." *Saints Herald* 126 (May 1, 1979): 7–8.

––––––. *Joseph Smith III: Pragmatic Prophet*. Urbana, Illinois: University of Illinois Press, 1988.

Madsen, Truman. *Joseph Smith the Prophet*. Salt Lake City, Utah: Bookcraft, Inc., 1989.

McKiernan, F. Mark. "David H. Smith: A Son of the Prophet." *BYU Studies* 18 (Winter 1978): 233–45.

Newell, Linda King, and Valeen Tippetts Avery. *Mormon Enigma: Emma Hale Smith*. Garden City, New York: Doubleday & Company, Inc., 1984.

Pardoe, T. Earl. *Lorin Farr, Pioneer*. Provo, Utah: Brigham Young University Press, 1953.

Poll, Richard D. "Joseph Smith and the Presidency, 1844." *Dialogue* 3 (Autumn 1968): 17–21.

Pratt, Parley P. *Autobiography of Parley P. Pratt*. Salt Lake City, Utah: Deseret Book Company, 1973.

Roberts, B.H. *The Life of John Taylor*. Salt Lake City, Utah: Bookcraft, Inc., 1963.

Rogers, Aurelia Spencer. *Life Sketches of Orson Spencer and Others, and History of Primary Work*. Salt Lake City, Utah: G.Q. Cannon and Sons, 1898.

Schindler, Harold. *Orrin Porter Rockwell: Man of God, Son of Thunder*. Salt Lake City: University of Utah Press, 1966.

Smith, Eliza R. Snow. *Biography and Family Record of Lorenzo Snow*. Salt Lake City, Utah: Deseret News Co., Printers, 1884.

Smith, Lucy Mack. *Biographical Sketches of Joseph Smith: The Prophet and His Progenitors for Many Generations*. New York: Arno Press, 1971.

Smith, Vida E. "Two Widows of the Brick Row." *Journal of History* 3 (April 1910): 202–12.

Van Wagoner, Richard S. "Sarah M. Pratt: The Shaping of an Apostate." *Dialogue* 19 (Summer 1986): 69–99.

———, and Steven C. Walker. *A Book of Mormons*. Salt Lake City: Signature Books, 1982.

Youngreen, Buddy. " 'Sons of the Martyrs' Nauvoo Reunion — 1860." *BYU Studies* 20 (Spring 1980): 351–70.

## Contemporary Accounts and Recollections

Adams, Henry. "Charles Francis Adams Visits the Mormons in 1844." *Proceedings of the Massachusetts Historical Society* 68 (1952): 267–300.

Allen, James B. " 'We Had A Very Hard Voyage for the Season': John Moon's Account of the First Emigrant Company of British Saints." *BYU Studies* 17 (Spring 1977): 339–40.

———."To the Saints in England: Impressions of a Mormon Immigrant (The 10 December 1840 William Clayton letter from Nauvoo to Manchester)." *BYU Studies* 18 (Spring 1978): 475–80.

———, and Thomas G. Alexander, eds. *Manchester Mormons: The Journal of William Clayton: 1840–1842*. Santa Barbara: Peregrine Smith, Inc., 1974.

Andrus, Hyrum L., and Helen Mae Andrus, comps. *They Knew the Prophet*. Salt Lake City, Utah: Bookcraft, Inc., 1974.

Beecher, Maureen Ursenbach. " 'All Things Move in Order in the City': The Nauvoo Diary of Zina Diantha Huntington Jacobs." *BYU Studies* 19 (Spring 1979): 285–320.

Bitton, Davis. *Guide to Mormon Diaries and Autobiographies*. Provo, Utah: Brigham Young University Press, 1977.

———. "Eliza R. Snow's Nauvoo Journal." *BYU Studies*, 15 (Summer 1975): 391–416.

Brooks, Juanita, ed. *On the Mormon Frontier: The Diary of Hosea Stout, 1844–1861*. 2 vols. Salt Lake City: University of Utah Press, 1964.

Cannon, Donald Q. "Reverend George Moore Comments on Nauvoo, the Mormons, and Joseph Smith." *Western Illinois Regional Studies* 5 (Spring 1982): 5–16.

Cook, Lyndon W. " 'A More Virtuous Man Never Existed on the Footstool of the Great Jehovah': George Miller on Joseph Smith." *BYU Studies* 19 (Spring 1979): 402–407.

———. " 'Brother Joseph Is Truly a Wonderful Man, He Is All We Could Wish a Prophet to Be': Pre-1844 Letters of William Law." *BYU Studies* 20 (Winter 1980): 207–218.

Ehat, Andrew F. " 'They Might Have Known That He Was Not a Fallen Prophet' — The Nauvoo Journal of Joseph Fielding." *BYU Studies* 19 (Winter 1979): 133–65.

_____, and Lyndon W. Cook, eds. *The Words of Joseph Smith.* Provo, Utah: Brigham Young University Religious Studies Center, 1980.

England, Eugene, ed. "George Laub's Nauvoo Journal." *BYU Studies* 18 (Winter 1978): 151–78.

Esplin, Ronald K. "Sickness and Faith, Nauvoo Letters." *BYU Studies* 15 (Summer 1975): 425–34.

_____."Life in Nauvoo, June 1844: Vilate Kimball's Martyrdom Letters." *BYU Studies* 19 (Winter 1979): 231–40.

Faulring, Scott H., ed. *An American Prophet's Record: The Diaries and Journals of Joseph Smith.* Salt Lake City, Utah: Signature Books, 1987.

Godfrey, Kenneth W., Audrey M. Godfrey, and Jill Mulvay Derr. *Women's Voices: An Untold History of the Latter-day Saints, 1830–1890.* Salt Lake City: Deseret Book Company, 1982.

Jennings, Warren A., ed. "Two Iowa Postmasters View Nauvoo: Anti-Mormon Letters to the Governor of Missouri." *BYU Studies* 11 (Spring 1971): 275–92.

Jessee, Dean. "Joseph Knight's Recollections of Early Mormon History." *BYU Studies* 16 (Autumn 1976): 29–39.

_____. "The Reliability of Joseph Smith's History." *Journal of Mormon History* 3 (1976): 23–46.

_____. "Howard Coray's Recollections of Joseph Smith." *BYU Studies* 17 (Spring 1977): 341–46.

_____. "Joseph Smith, Jr.—In His Own Words." *Ensign* 15 (February 1985): 6–13.

_____, ed. *The Personal Writings of Joseph Smith.* Salt Lake City, Utah: Deseret Book Company, 1983.

_____, ed. "The John Taylor Nauvoo Journal, January 1845–September 1845." *BYU Studies* 23 (Summer 1983): 1–124.

_____, ed. *The Papers of Joseph Smith: Autobiographical and Historical Writings.* Vol.1. Salt Lake City, Utah: Deseret Book Company, 1989.

Kenney, Scott G., ed. *Wilford Woodruff's Journals: 1833–1898 Typescript.* 9 vols. Midvale, Utah: Signature Books, 1983.

Kimball, Stanley B., ed. *On the Potter's Wheel: The Diaries of Heber C. Kimball.* Salt Lake City, Utah: Signature Books, 1987.

Larmer, Rev. Father John. "Catholic Church in McDonough County." In *History of McDonough County*, edited by G. J. Clarke, Springfield, Illinois: D. W. Lusk, State Printer, 1978.

Lyon, T. Edgar. " 'Recollections of Old Nauvooers' Memories from Oral History." *BYU Studies* 18 (Winter 1978): 143–50.

Marsh, E. Baldwin. "Mormons in Hancock County: A Reminiscence." *Journal of Illinois State Historical Society* 64 (Spring 1971): 22–65.

Mulder, William, and A. Russell Mortensen, eds. *Among the Mormons: Historic Accounts by Contemporary Observers.* New York: Alfred A. Knopf, 1969.

Quincy, Josiah. *Figures of the Past*. Boston: Little, Brown, and Co., 1926.

Robinson, Ebenezer. "Items of Personal History of the Editor." *The Return* (May–July 1890).

Searle, Howard C. "Authorship of the History of Joseph Smith: A Review Essay." *BYU Studies* 21 (Winter 1981): 101–122.

Ursenbach, Maureen. "The Iowa Journal of Lorenzo Snow." *BYU Studies* (Summer 1984): 261–73.

Watson, Elden Jay, ed. *Manuscript History of Brigham Young: 1801–1844*. Salt Lake City, Utah: Smith Secretarial Service, 1968.

———, ed. *Manuscript History of Brigham Young: 1846–1847*. Salt Lake City: Elden J. Watson, 1971.

———, ed. *The Orson Pratt Journals*. Salt Lake City: Elden J. Watson, 1975.

## Doctrinal Development in Nauvoo

Allen, James B. "Line Upon Line." *Ensign* 9 (July 1979): 32–39.

Ashment, Edward H. "The Book of Abraham Facsimiles: A Reappraisal." *Sunstone* 4 (December 1979): 33–48.

Bishop, M. Guy. "To Overcome the 'Last Enemy': Early Mormon Perceptions of Death." *BYU Studies* 26 (Summer 1986): 63–79.

Blair, Alma R. "RLDS Views of Polygamy: Some Historiographical Notes." *The John Whitmer Historical Association Journal* 5 (1985): 16–28.

Buerger, David John. "The Development of the Mormon Temple Endowment Ceremony." *Dialogue* 20 (Winter 1987): 33–76.

———. " 'The Fulness of the Priesthood': The Second Anointing in Latter-day Saint Theology and Practice." *Dialogue* 16 (Spring 1983): 10–44.

Cannon, Donald Q. "The King Follett Discourse: Joseph Smith's Greatest Sermon in Historical Perspective." *BYU Studies* 18 (Winter 1978): 179–92.

Conrad, Larry W., and Paul Shupe. "An RLDS Reformation: Construing the Task of RLDS Theology." *Dialogue* 18 (Summer 1985): 92–103.

Cook, Lyndon W. *The Revelations of the Prophet Joseph Smith: A Historical and Biographical Commentary of the Doctrine and Covenants*. Salt Lake City, Utah: Deseret Book, 1985.

Ehat, Andrew F. "It Seems Like Heaven Began on Earth: Joseph Smith and the Constitution of the Kingdom of God." *BYU Studies* 20 (Spring 1980): 253–80.

Foster, Lawrence. *Religion and Sexuality: Three American Communal Experiments of the Nineteenth Century*. New York: Oxford University Press, 1981.

Godfrey, Kenneth W. "A New Look at the Alleged Little Known Discourse by Joseph Smith." *BYU Studies* 9 (Autumn 1968): 49–53.

Goodyear, Imogene. "Joseph Smith and Polygamy: An Alternative View." *John Whitmer History Association* 4 (1984): 16–21.

Hale, Van. "The Doctrinal Impact of the King Follett Discourse." *BYU Studies* 18 (Winter 1978): 209–25.

Ham, Wayne. *Publish Glad Tidings: Readings in Early Latter Day Saint Sources.* Independence, Mo.: Herald Publishing House, 1970.

Harrell, Charles R. "The Development of the Doctrine of Preexistence, 1830–1844." *BYU Studies* 28 (Spring 1988): 75–96.

Heath, Steven H. "The Sacred Shout." *Dialogue* 19 (Fall 1986): 115–23.

Howard, Richard P. "The Changing RLDS Response to Mormon Polygamy: A Preliminary Analysis." *The John Whitmer Historical Association Journal* 3 (1983): 14–28.

Irving, Gordon. "The Law of Adoption: One Phase of the Development of the Mormon Concept of Salvation, 1830–1900." *BYU Studies* 14 (Spring 1974): 291–314.

Larson, Stan. "The King Follett Discourse: A Newly Amalgamated Text." *BYU Studies* 18 (Winter 1978): 193–208.

Lyon, T. Edgar. "Nauvoo and the Council of the Twelve." In *The Restoration Movement: Essays in Mormon History*, edited by F. Mark McKiernan, Alma R. Blair and Paul M. Edwards, 167–206. Lawrence, Kansas: Coronado Press, 1973.

———. "Doctrinal Development of the Church During the Nauvoo Sojourn, 1839–1846." *BYU Studies* 15 (Summer 1975): 435–445.

Madsen, Truman G., ed. *Concordance of Doctrinal Statements of Joseph Smith.* Salt Lake City, Utah: I.E.F. Publishing, 1985.

Matthews, Robert J. "The Bernhisel Manuscript Copy of Joseph Smith's inspired Version of the Bible." *BYU Studies* 11 (Spring 1971): 253–274.

———. *"A Plainer Translation": Joseph Smith's Translation of the Bible, A History and Commentary.* Provo, Utah: Brigham Young University Press, 1975.

Ostler, Blake. "The Idea of Pre-existence in the Development of Mormon Thought." *Dialogue* 15 (Spring 1982): 59–78.

Paul, Robert E. "Joseph Smith and the Plurality of Worlds Idea." *Dialogue* 19 (Summer 1986): 12–38.

Quinn, D. Michael. "The Evolution of the Presiding Quorums of the LDS Church." *Journal of Mormon History* 1 (1971): 21–38.

———. "The Practice of Rebaptism at Nauvoo." *BYU Studies* 18 (Winter 1978): 226–32.

———. "Latter-day Prayer Circles." *BYU Studies* 19 (Fall 1978): 79–105.

———. "The Council of Fifty and Its Members, 1844 to 1945." *BYU Studies* 20 (Winter 1980): 163–97.

Smith, Joseph, Jr. *Teachings of the Prophet Joseph Smith.* Joseph Fielding Smith, comp. Salt Lake City, Utah: Deseret Book Company, 1976.

Underwood, Grant. "Book of Mormon Usage in Early LDS Theology." *Dialogue* 17 (Autumn 1984): 35–74.

Van Orden, Bruce A. "Items of Instruction: Section 130 and 131." In *Harken O Ye People*. 231–47. Salt Lake City, Utah: Randall Book Company, 1984.

Van Wagoner, Richard S. *Mormon Polygamy: A History*. Salt Lake City, Utah: Signature Books, 1986.

Welch, John W., and David J. Whittaker, " 'We Believe. . . . ': Development of the Articles of Faith." *Ensign* 9 (September 1979): 50–55.

**Individual Sites**

Anderson, Paul L. "Heroic Nostalgia: Enshrining the Mormon Past." *Sunstone* 5 (July–August 1980): 47–55.

Arrington, Joseph Earl. "Destruction of the Mormon Temple at Nauvoo." *Journal of the Illinois State Historical Society* 40 (1947): 414–25.

Berge, Dale L. *Archaeology of the Daniel Butler, Jr., Property, Nauvoo, Illinois*. Nauvoo: Nauvoo Restoration, Inc., 1979.

_____. "The Jonathan Browning Site: An Example of Archaeology for Restoration in Nauvoo, Illinois." *BYU Studies* 19 (Winter 1979): 201–28.

Bray, Robert T. *Times and Seasons: An Archaeological Perspective on Early Latter Day Saints Printing*. Columbia: University of Missouri Press, 1976.

_____. *Archeology at the Joseph Smith Stable, Southwest Corner Water and Carlin Streets, Nauvoo, Illinois*. Columbia: University of Missouri Press, 1980.

_____. *The Turley Site: An Account of the 1973 Archaeological Work, Nauvoo, Illinois*. Columbia, Missouri: University of Missouri Press, 1980.

Brigham, Janet. "Nauvoo Today: Building Again the City Beautiful." *Ensign* 10 March 1980): 44–47.

Brown, Lisle G. "The Sacred Departments for Temple Work in Nauvoo: The Assembly Room and the Council Chamber." *BYU Studies* 19 (Spring 1979): 361–74.

Harrington, Virginia S., and J. C. Harrington, *Rediscovery of the Nauvoo Temple: Report on Archaeological Excavations*. Salt Lake City: Nauvoo Restoration, Inc., 1971.

Historic Sites Committee. *Historic Sites and Structures of Hancock County, Illinois*. Carthage: Hancock County Historical Society, 1979.

Jackson, Richard H. "The Mormon Village: Genesis and Antecedents of the City of Zion Plan." *BYU Studies* 17 (Winter 1977): 223–40.

_____, and Roger Henrie. "Perceptions of Sacred Space." *Journal of Cultural Geography* 3 (Spring–Summer 1983): 94–107.

Johnson, Randy. "Seventeen Historical Sites Dedicated in Nauvoo, Ill." *Ensign* 12 (October 1982): 74–76.

Kimball, Stanley B. "The Nauvoo Temple." *The Improvement Era* 66 (November, 1963): 974–984.

Launius, Roger D., and F. Mark McKiernan. *Joseph Smith Jr.'s Red Brick Store*. Macomb, Illinois: Western Illinois University, 1985.

McKiernan, F. Mark. *A Master Plan of the Historic Properties of the RLDS Church: Preserving and Interpreting Our Physical Heritage*. n.p., n.d.

McRae, Joseph and Eunice McRae. *Historic Facts Concerning the Liberty and Carthage Jails*. Salt Lake City, Utah: Utah Printing, 1954.

Peatross, C. Ford. *Historic America: Buildings, Structures, and Sites*. Washington D.C.: Library of Congress, 1983.

Shaffer, Donald R. "The Hiram Clark Home—Nauvoo." *Restoration Trails Forum* 14 (March 1988): 6–8.

Siegfried, Mark H. "Description of Historic Places in Nauvoo." *Journal of History* 13 (January 1920): 1–8.

Stobaugh, Kenneth. "The Historic Site: A Document of the Past." *Saints Herald* 124 (October 1977): 31–34.

Taylor, James C. and Donna Taylor. *Nauvoo Death and Burial: Old Nauvoo Burial Ground*. Nauvoo, Ill.: Nauvoo Restoration Inc., 1989.

**Photography and Nauvoo**

Francis, Rell G. *The Utah Photographs of George Edward Anderson*. Lincoln, Nebraska: University of Nebraska Press, 1979.

Kimball, James L. Jr., and Jed Clark. "The Way It Looks Today: A Camera Tour of Church History Sites in Illinois." *Ensign* 9 (September 1979): 34–50.

Tobler, Douglas S., and Nelson B. Wadsworth. *The History of the Mormons in Photographs and Text: 1832 to the Present*. New York: St. Martins Press, 1989.

Wadsworth, Nelson B. *Through Camera Eyes*. Provo, Utah: Brigham Young University Press, 1975.

**Specialized Studies**

Bishop, Guy, Vincent Lacey, and Richard Wixom. "Death at Mormon Nauvoo, 1843–1845." *Western Illinois Regional Studies* 19 (Fall 1986): 71–77.

———. "Sex Roles, Marriage, and Childbearing at Mormon Nauvoo." *Western Illinois Regional Studies* 11 (Fall 1988): 30–45.

Bunker, Gary L. and Davis Bitton. *The Mormon Graphic Image, 1834–1914: Cartoons, Caricatures, and Illustrations*. Salt Lake City: University of Utah Press, 1983.

Cannon, Donald Q. "Spokes on the Wheel: Early Latter-day Settlements in Hancock County, Illinois." *Ensign* 15 (February 1986): 62–68.

Cannon, M. Hamlin. "Migration of English Mormons to America." *American Historical Review* 52 (1946–47): 436–55.

Coates, Lawrence G. "Brigham Young and Mormon Indian Policies: The Formative Period, 1836–1851." *BYU Studies* 18 (Spring 1978): 428–52.

Cook, Lyndon. *Civil Marriages in Nauvoo and Some Outlying Areas: 1839–1845*. Provo, Utah: Liberty Press, 1980.

Enders, Donald L. "The Steamboat Maid of Iowa: Mormon Mistress of the Mississippi." *BYU Studies* 19 (Spring 1979): 321–35.

_____. "A Dam for Nauvoo: An Attempt to Industrialize the City." *BYU Studies* 18 (Winter 1978): 246–54.

Firmage, Edwin Brown and Richard Collin Mangrun. *Zion in the Courts: A Legal History of The Church of Jesus Christ of Latter-day Saints 1830–1900.* Urbana: University of Illinois Press, 1988.

Flake, Chad J., ed. *A Mormon Bibliography 1830–1930: Books, Pamphlets, Periodicals, and Broadsheets.* Salt Lake City: University of Utah Press, 1978.

Godfrey, Kenneth W. "Joseph Smith and the Masons." *Journal of Illinois State Historical Society* 64 (Spring 1971): 79–90.

_____. "A Note on the Nauvoo Library and Literary Society." *BYU Studies* 14 (Spring 1974): 386–88.

_____. "Some Thoughts Regarding an Unwritten History of Nauvoo." *BYU Studies* 15 (Summer 1975): 417–24.

_____. "The Nauvoo Neighborhood: A Little Philadelphia or a Unique City Set Upon a Hill." *Journal of Mormon History* 11 (1984): 79–98.

Hansen, Klaus J. *The Political Kingdom of God and The Council of Fifty in Mormon History.* Lincoln, Nebraska: University of Nebraska Press, 1967.

Hartley, William G. "Joseph Smith and Nauvoo's Youth." *Ensign* 9 (September 1979): 26–29.

Hicks, Michael. "Poetic Borrowing in Early Mormonism." *Dialogue* 18 (Spring 1985): 132–44.

_____. *Mormonism and Music: A History.* Urbana, Illinois: University of Illinois Press, 1989.

Hogan, Mervin B. *Founding Minutes of the Nauvoo Lodge, U.D..* Des Moines, Iowa: Research Lodge Number 2, 1971.

Holbrook, Leona. "Dancing as an Aspect of Early Mormon and Utah Culture." *BYU Studies* 16 (Autumn 1975): 117–38.

Jolley, Jerry C. "The Sting of the *Wasp*: Early Nauvoo Newspaper—April 1842 to April 1843." *BYU Studies* 22 (Fall 1982): 487–96.

Kimball, James L., Jr. "A Wall to Defend Zion: The Nauvoo Charter." *BYU Studies* 15 (Summer 1975): 491–97.

Launius, Roger D. "Anti-Mormonism in Illinois: Thomas C. Sharp's Unfinished History of the Mormon War, 1845." *Journal of Mormon History* 15 (1989): 27–46.

Lyon, T. Edgar. "Free Masonry at Nauvoo." *Dialogue* 6 (Spring 1971): 76–78.

_____. "The Account Books of the Amos Davis Store at Commerce, Illinois." *BYU Studies* 19 (Winter 1979): 241–43.

Moody, Thurmon Dean. "Nauvoo's Whistling and Whittling Brigade." *BYU Studies* 15 (Summer 1975): 480–90.

Oaks, Dallin H. "The Suppression of the Nauvoo Expositor." *Utah Law Review* 9 (Winter 1965): 862–903.

_____, and Joseph I. Bentley. "Joseph Smith and Legal Process: In the Wake of the Steamboat Nauvoo." *BYU Law Review* 19 (Winter 1979): 167–99.

Rowley, Dennis. "Nauvoo: A River Town." *BYU Studies* 18 (Winter 1978): 255–72.

Rust, Alvin E. *Mormon and Utah Coin and Currency*. Salt Lake City, Utah: Rust Rare Coins, Inc., 1984.

Schweikart, Larry. "The Mormon Connection: Lincoln, Saints, and the Crisis of Equality." *Western Humanities Review* 34 (Winter 1980): 1–22.

Smith, James. "Frontier Nauvoo: Building a Picture from Statistics." *Ensign* 9 (September 1979): 16–19.

Sonne, Conway B. *Ships, Saints, and Mariners: A Maritime Encyclopedia of Mormon Migration, 1830–1890*. Salt Lake City: University of Utah Press, 1987.

Tanner, Terence A. "The Mormon Press in Nauvoo, 1839–1846." *Western Illinois Regional Studies* 11 (Fall 1988): 5–27.

Underwood, Grant. "Early Mormon Perceptions of Contemporary America, 1830–1846." *BYU Studies* 26 (Summer 1986): 49–61.

———. "Apocalyptic Adversaries: Mormonism Meets Millerism." *John Whitmer Historical Association Journal* 7 (1987): 53–61.

Watson, Elden J. "The Nauvoo Tabernacle." *BYU Studies* 19 (Spring 1979): 416–21.

Whittaker, David. "Early Mormon Pamphleteering 1836–1857." *Journal of Mormon History* 4 (1977): 35–49.

**Women's Studies**

Arrington, Leonard B. "Persons for All Seasons: Women in Mormon History." *BYU Studies* 20 (Fall 1979): 39–58.

Beecher, Maureen Ursenbach, and Lavina Fielding Anderson, eds. *Sisters in Spirit: Mormon Women in Historical and Cultural Perspective*. Urbana: University of Illinois Press, 1987.

Madsen, Carol C., and David J. Whittaker. "History's Sequel: A Source Essay on Women in Mormon History." *Journal of Mormon History* 6 (1979): 123–45.

Burgess-Olson, Vicky. *Sister Saints*. Provo, Utah: Brigham Young University Press, 1978.

Scott, Anne Firor. "Mormon Women, Other Women: Paradoxes and Challenges." *Journal of Mormon History* 13 (1986–87): 3–20.

Scott, Lyn, and Maureen Ursenbach Beecher. "Mormon Women: A Bibliography in Process, 1977–1985." *Journal of Mormon History* 12 (1985): 113–27.

Ursenbach, Maureen, and James L. Kimball, Jr. "The First Relief Society." *Ensign* 9 (March 1979): 25–29.

# MARTYRDOM

Barnett, Steven G. "The Canes of the Martyrdom." *BYU Studies* 21 (Spring 1981): 205–11.

Bitton, Davis. "The Martyrdom of Joseph Smith in Early Mormon Writings." *The John Whitmer Historical Association Journal* 3 (1983): 29–39.

Dennis, Ronald D., trans. "The Martyrdom of Joseph Smith and His Brother Hyrum by Dan Jones." *BYU Studies* 24 (Winter 1984): 78–109.

Ellsworth, Paul D. "Mobocracy and the Rule of Law: American Press Reaction to the Murder of Joseph Smith." *BYU Studies* 20 (Fall 1979): 71–82.

Gayler, George W. "Governor Ford and the Death of Joseph and Hiram Smith." *Journal of the Illinois State Historical Society* 50 (1957): 391–411.

Godfrey, Kenneth W. "Non-Mormon Views of the Martyrdom: A Look at Some Early Published Accounts." *The John Whitmer Historical Association Journal* 7 (1987): 12–20.

Hicks, Michael. " 'Strains Which Will Not Soon Be Allowed to Die . . . ':'The Stranger' and Carthage Jail." *BYU Studies* 23 (Fall 1983): 389–400.

Jessee, Dean C. "Return to Carthage: Writing the History of Joseph Smith's Martyrdom." *Journal of Mormon History* 8 (1981): 3–20.

Oaks, Dallin H., and Marvin S. Hill. *Carthage Conspiracy: The Trial of the Accused Assassins of Joseph Smith*. Urbana, Illinois: University of Illinois Press, 1976.

Shipps, Jan. "A Little Known Account of the Murders of Joseph and Hyrum Smith." *BYU Studies* 14 (Spring 1974): 389–92.

Van Wagoner, Richard, and Steven C. Walker. "The Joseph/Hyrum Smith Funeral Sermon." *BYU Studies* 23 (Winter 1983): 3–18.

# SUCCESSION CRISIS

Bates, Irene M. "William Smith, 1811-1893: Problematic Patriarch." *Dialogue* 18 (Summer 1983): 11–23.

Durham, Reed C., and Steven H. Heath. *Succession in the Church*. Salt Lake City, Utah: Deseret Book Company, 1964.

Edwards, Paul. "William B. Smith: The Persistent 'Pretender.' " *Dialogue* 18 (Summer 1985): 128–39.

Esplin, Ronald K. "Joseph, Brigham and the Twelve: A Succession of Continuity." *BYU Studies* 21 (Summer 1981): 301–41.

Launius, Roger. "Joseph Smith III and the Mormon Succession Crisis, 1844-1846." *Western Illinois Regional Studies* 6 (Spring 1983): 5–22.

McMurray, W. Grant. "True Son of a True Father: Joseph Smith III and the Succession Question." In *Restoration Studies: A Collection of Essays About the History, Beliefs, and Practices of the Reorganized Church of Jesus Christ of Latter-Day Saints*, vol.1, edited by Maurice L. Draper, 131–45. Independence, Missouri: Temple School, 1980.

Quinn, D. Michael. "The Mormon Succession Crisis of 1844." *BYU Studies* 16 (Winter 1976): 187–233.

Russell, William. "King James Strang: Joseph Smith Successor?" In *The Restoration Movement: Essays in Mormon History*, edited by F. Mark McKiernan, Alma R. Blair and Paul M. Edwards, 231–56. Lawrence, Kansas: Coronado Press, 1973.

Shields, Steven L. *Divergent Paths of the Restoration*. Bountiful, Utah: Restoration Research, 1982.

―――. *The Latter-Day Saint Churches: An Annotated Bibliography*. New York: Garland Publishing, Inc., 1987.

# EXODUS

Brown, Joseph E. *The Mormon Trek West: The Journey of American Exiles*. Garden City, New York: Doubleday & Company, Inc., 1980.

Clayton, William. *William Clayton: Journal: A Daily Record of the Journey of the Original Company of "Mormons" Pioneers from Nauvoo, Ill., to The Valley of the Great Salt Lake*. Salt Lake City, Utah: Deseret News Press, 1921.

Esplin, Ronald K. "A Place Prepared: Joseph, Brigham and the Quest for Promised Refuge in the West." *Journal of Mormon History* 9 (1982): 85–111.

Pruday, William E. "They March Their Way West: The Nauvoo Brass Band." *Ensign* 10 (July 1980): 20–23.

Rich, Russell. *Ensign to the Nations: History of the LDS Church from 1846–1972*. Provo, Utah: Brigham Young University Press, 1973.

# INDEX

Nauvoo Temple Star Stone fragment.
Photograph courtesy of Harold Allen.

# ABOUT THE AUTHORS

T. Jeffery Cottle, a descendant of Nauvoo Mormon pioneers, practices law in Orem, Utah. Before receiving his law degree from Lewis and Clark Law School in Portland, Oregon, he studied anthropology and public administration at Brigham Young University. This book resulted from his interests in photography and Mormon history. He lives in Provo, Utah, with his wife, Michaela Voss Cottle.

Richard Neitzel Holzapfel teaches for the LDS Church Educational System. He studied political science at Brigham Young University and history at California State University, Fullerton, and at the University of California, Irvine. He has spent many years researching Mormon history, learning the history of architecture and photography in the process. He lives in Irvine, California, with his wife, Jeni Broberg Holzapfel, and their five children.

Jeff and Richard have collaborated on several articles, and the second book in this series entitled *Old Mormon Palmyra and New England: Historic Photographs and Guide* (Santa Ana: Fieldbrook Productions, Inc., 1991).